ADVANCE PRAISE

Authors Weiss and Schneider capture the essence of how rapidly technology is changing arousal and attachment patterns and what you can do about it. This is sure to become the book that both clinicians and lay readers turn to in order to sort out the complexities of how technology turns us on.

—Dr. Kenneth M. Adams, author of *Silently Seduced: When Parents Make Their Children Partners* and *When He's Married to Mom: How to Help Mother Enmeshed Men Open Their Hearts to True Love and Commitment* and co-editor of *Clinical Management of Sex Addiction*

Always Turned On is packed with the most up-to-date information about sex addiction in the digital age. It's non-shaming, encouraging tone shows not only the addict, but also partners that recovery is possible. The resources and practical advice offered by the authors is excellent for addicts that are new to recovery and their partners.

—Dr. Stefanie Carnes, author of *Mending a Shattered Heart: A Guide for Partners of Sex Addicts, Facing Addiction: Starting Recovery from Alcohol and Drugs,* and *Facing Heartbreak: Steps to Recovery for Partners of Sex Addicts*

Weiss and Schneider are two of the world's leading experts on how technology is shifting our understanding of human sexuality. *Always Turned On* provides insights and solutions for when sexual addiction meets the digital age.

—Dr. David Delmonico, professor of counseling at Duquesne University, and co-author of *In the Shadows of the Net, Cybersex Unplugged,* and *Illegal Images*

Always Turned On is compact, comprehensive and consistently engaging to read. It is now one of my "go to" books for guidance and just plain good advice about cybersex addiction. Great work; great resource!

—Dr. Pat Love, author, *The Truth about Love: The Highs, the Lows, and How You Can Make It Last Forever*

Sex, love and romance are delightful aspects of our humanity and a necessary part of the mating game. But what happens when these gifts of life become nothing more than a game somebody uses compulsively at the expense of deepening relationships or to medicate themselves? The authors do an excellent job of explaining how sex and romance can become addictive, why it is on the increase, and how to get back to healthy intimacy.

—Dr. Brenda Schaeffer, Licensed Psychologist, Certified Addiction Specialist, and author of *Is It Love or Is It Addiction?*

ALWAYS TURNED ON

SEX ADDICTION IN THE DIGITAL AGE

ALWAYS TURNED ON

SEX ADDICTION IN THE DIGITAL AGE

ROBERT WEISS, LCSW, CSAT-S

JENNIFER SCHNEIDER, MD, PhD

Gentle Path
P R E S S

Gentle Path Press
P.O. Box 3172
Carefree, Arizona 85377
gentlepath.com
Copyright © 2015 by Gentle Path Press

First edition: 2015

For more information regarding our publications, please contact Gentle Path Press at 1-800-708-1796 (toll-free U.S. only)

ISBN: 978-0-9850633-6-8

Editor's note: All the stories in this book are based on actual experiences. The names and details have been changed to protect the privacy of people involved. In some cases, composites have been created. Any resemblance to actual persons is entirely coincidental.

We dedicate this book to those who seek soothing and emotional solace through the abuse of pornography and casual sex. Our hope is that by reading this book, they may begin to find their way to genuine healing, intimacy, and connection.

We also dedicate this book to Jessica Grace Wing (1971–2003) beloved daughter of co-author Jennifer Schneider.

ACKNOWLEDGMENTS

Robert Weiss

First, I want to acknowledge the incredibly supportive management team at Elements Behavioral Health. David, Rob, Keith, Vera (and too many others to name here), you have set a platform in place for me. Our work together allows me to shine on every level and I am endlessly appreciative. Thanks to my ever patient husband Jon, who helps me see past today's fleeting free moments to when we will have more time to share and enjoy our lives together. Thanks to Corrine Casanova, Tami VerHelst and Stefanie Carnes at the International Institute of Trauma and Addiction Professionals for making the publication of this book possible. Jennifer and I could not do what we do without the support of researcher, author, editor, Scott Brassart. A special shout out to Laura Maxey and Diana Lombardi of 5WPR who work so hard to make sure the world has a chance to hear and read these words of healing. And finally, to those who seek sexual healing and recovery read on, your answers await you and then you can start recreating your life as you wish it to be.

Jennifer Schneider

I would like to acknowledge the support of Marni Dittmar, Lucia Yao, and David Sims, librarians at the Tucson Medical Center Library. Without their willingness to send me dozens of references on short notice, I could not possibly have accomplished the research and writing that I contributed to this book. And thank you to Debra Kaplan for many relevant conversations as well as a review of this material. I would also like to acknowledge my late daughter Jessica Grace Wing, a big participant in the early days of the Internet revolution and one of the first volunteer "digital natives." I wish she could have lived to see how the Internet has changed the world.

CONTENTS

AUTHORS' NOTE

This is not a book about morality, cultural beliefs, cultural norms, or religion. It is not written to challenge those who enjoy porn use and other tech-driven forms of sexuality either casually or as a lifestyle. As mental health and addiction professionals it is not our job to judge human behavior in any way. Instead, we have written this book to help people whose porn use, sexual hookups, and the like have escalated to the point where those activities have become a driving life force at the expense of their own personal beliefs, morality, and lifestyle. In other words, this book is written for those whose abusive or addictive involvement with online porn and non-intimate sex (via apps and the Internet) consistently and persistently distracts them from larger personal goals like academic achievement, career development, family, intimate relationships, recreation, and community. Within these pages we offer understanding, compassion, direction, and hope to those too ashamed, fearful, or embarrassed to reach out in other ways.

Although there are many views about whether pornography, virtual sex, and casual/anonymous sex are "wrong" or "right"—along with a multitude of moral, ethical, and religious beliefs on the subject—it is not the intent of this book to define or address these issues in any meaningful way. The authors support every adult in his or her right to engage in any solo or mutually consensual (and legal) sexual activity or experience that provides pleasure, satisfaction, and fulfillment. We do not believe that we or anyone else has the right to judge what turns someone on or how a person pursues sexual activity, as long as that person's choices do not violate the intrinsic rights and safety of themselves or others. Our work is not focused on what is ethically, religiously, or politically correct for any individual or the culture at large. We do not promote censorship, nor do we believe that all pornography is problematic or exploitative, though some certainly can be—child porn most assuredly.

Our primary goal within these pages is to assist people who struggle with compulsive sexual behaviors, especially when those behaviors are tech-driven, helping them to identify their problem as the chronic emotional disorder it is and to understand that it can be put into remission with proper care and direction—just like alcoholism, gambling addiction, or drug addiction. In a nutshell, we want people who are suffering from sexual addiction to know that their sexual concerns can be addressed without shame, moral, or cultural bias. We also seek to offer direction and insight to therapists and other professionals who may be unfamiliar with the treatment of sex addiction. But most of all, we want to offer cybersex addicts hope, letting them know that long-term change and healing are possible.

PREFACE

As the twentieth century came to a close, noting an increase in sexual problems related to newly evolving technologies like personal computers and the Internet, the authors of this work wrote a now out-of-print book called *Cybersex Exposed*.[1] That book, at the time the only public-facing work on the topic, was read and utilized almost exclusively by cybersex addicts and the clinicians treating them, and this was in fact our intended audience. Since that time, in conjunction with various technological advances, many new challenges to intimacy, sexuality, and relationships have emerged.

By 2006, tech had moved so far and so fast that we felt compelled to write a similarly focused but dramatically updated book called *Untangling the Web: Sex, Porn, and Fantasy Obsession in the Internet Age*.[2] *Untangling the Web* quickly replaced *Cybersex Exposed* as an up-to-date and useful book for digital-age sex addicts, their families, and sex addiction treatment specialists.

Untangling the Web focused on the tech-driven sexual problems of its era. Much of that book was devoted to online pornography—the ways in which it was accessed, used, and abused. We also included information about the obsessive online search for live sexual encounters and romantic relationships, which then occurred primarily through chat rooms, dating websites (Match.com and eHarmony), and hookup websites (Craigslist and Backpage).

Over the years both *Cybersex Exposed* and *Untangling the Web* reached and helped many people and we're proud of that. But that was then and this is now. With each increasingly swift turn of the technological wheel, the problem of Internet-related sexual addiction has escalated—seemingly at an almost unfathomable pace. For starters, Facebook, Twitter, Instagram, Tumblr, Snapchat, and other forms of social media have all "arrived" in the last five years or so, as have smartphones, texting/sexting, dating/hookup apps, ubiquitous GPS technology, selfies, video chat, and more. So, needless to say, it is time for another take on digitally driven challenges to intimacy, sexuality, and relationships.

Somewhat embarrassingly, we initially thought that a modest update to *Untangling the Web* was in order. Wow, were we wrong about that. Rather quickly into the research and rewrite process it became apparent that a "brief revision" was not going to cut it and an entirely new book was needed. That new book, steeped in our past experience with sexual addiction and intimacy disorders treatment and our burgeoning understanding of the ways in which technology affects human relationships,[3] is the volume you are now reading.

Way back in 1998 when *Cybersex Exposed* was written, the number of people who owned or had access to computers either at home or at work was rapidly increasing, as was the number of people challenged by their abuse of cybersex. In recognizing this, we were on the cutting edge of our professions. We also thought we were pretty cool for using and helping to define the freshly minted term "cybersex," referring to it as the use of home and/or work computers to access porn, casual sex, and/or prostitutes. Now this vision and definition is merely antiquated.

Today cybersex activities are carried out primarily using portable electronic devices—laptops, tablets, and smartphones—and the types of imagery and activity accessed for sexual and romantic pleasure are pretty much endless. Furthermore, new technologies creating new forms of sexual experiences arise almost daily. Sexting, the process of sending nude or nearly nude pictures to partners or potential partners, is now commonplace, user-generated pornography is ubiquitous, Facebook has over a billion active users,[4] and many other social networking sites are increasing in popularity. And thanks to an advertising-based business model initially employed by newspapers, television, and radio, nearly all of this content is today provided at little or no cost to the user. This means that almost anyone can instantly and affordably access an endless stream of explicit sexual content and willing sexual partners—all by simply tapping an electronically sensitive glass surface. Not surprisingly, for some people this nearly unlimited access to highly stimulating sexual content and activity is both contributing to and exacerbating cybersex addiction.

Obviously, being sexual is not problematic for most people, just as drinking alcohol, eating cake, and gambling are not problematic for most people. However, as long as specific substances and behaviors have the capacity to evoke profound pleasure and distraction, a small percentage of people will abuse those pleasures as a way to establish external control over difficult internal emotions and experiences. These people learn to abuse flirting and sex, gaming and gambling, spending, eating, and/or alcohol and drugs as a way to disconnect and dissociate from uncomfortable emotions and life stressors—eventually finding themselves hooked on the pleasurable escape that these experiences offer. In other words, these people use addictive substances and/or behaviors not for enjoyment, but as a means of escaping or controlling what they feel. Sex and the search for sex as a pleasurable distraction is no exception to this process.

Note: Throughout this book we will use the terms "sexual addiction," "sexual compulsivity," and "hypersexuality" interchangeably. As of now, there is no officially preferred term for identifying and/or describing sexual addiction, so we feel it is best to incorporate all of the language in common use.

The basics of sexual addiction remain the same with or without technology. Sex addicts have always engaged in their problematic sexual "behaviors of choice" compulsively and to their detriment. Oftentimes they do so despite clearly related negative life consequences. As a result, their existing relationships slowly crumble, school and work become a struggle, and they simultaneously lose interest in recreation, hobbies, and other activities they once enjoyed. Sex addicts isolate, they experience debilitating shame about their sexual activities, their emotional and physical health suffers, they get arrested, and lose hope. Many sex addicts make promises to themselves or others that they will stop engaging in their troubling behavior, only to find themselves back in the same or similar patterns just a short time later. This is the "loss of control" or "powerlessness" inherent in all forms of addiction. In these respects, the internal emotional challenges of sex addiction are the same as ever. The fact that in today's world digital technology so thoroughly facilitates this effort is merely a by-product of the modern age. What has changed most profoundly in recent years is the manner and speed with which sex addicts can locate and access the content and partners that fuel their addictions.

As this text unfolds, we will describe in detail what constitutes cybersex and addiction. We will look at how digital technology can facilitate obsessive patterns of sexual fantasy and behavior. We will also examine cybersex addiction from the perspective of the spouse or partner of the addict and the addict's family. Also included is material for parents concerned about the online sexual behavior of their children, many of whom, via technology, are either intentionally accessing or inadvertently being exposed to age-inappropriate sexual material and advances.

This book is based on actual clinical experience, research, and inter-actions we have had with people seeking help. We have highlighted spe-cific issues, changed names, and combined tales to both underscore the topic being examined and to protect the identities of the persons involved. But overall what is written represents the people and the real problems we encounter in our professional lives every day.

If you are seeking information about and/or relief from addictive sexual behaviors for yourself, for a loved one, or for a client, this book is for you. It doesn't matter if you are married or single, male or female, straight or gay, or anything in between. If your life has been adversely affected by your own or someone else's digitally driven compulsive sexual behavior, then the information contained herein can help you to recognize, understand, and heal your problem.

INTRODUCTION

DIGITAL TECHNOLOGY AND OUR EVER-CHANGING WORLD

When I was in school, it took me two days to type my senior term paper. Every time I made a typing error, it took me about five minutes to fix it. And this was after I'd spent twenty or thirty hours in the school library, poring over the card catalog. Yesterday my granddaughter started her paper at 9 a.m., and she was done by 3 p.m. Her research took about twenty minutes, and any changes she wanted to make took about half a second. As a grandmother, I don't know if I'm in love with digital technology, but I sure would've liked it when I was in high school.

—Martha, sixty-four, grandmother

When I was a kid, my dad worked overseas for three months at a time. Home for a month, gone for three; home for a month, gone for three. We sent letters back and forth every week, but most of the time it felt like he wasn't a real part of our family. And I know that my mom really felt abandoned. Today, I'm in the armed forces serving overseas, and it's totally different for me and my family. I see my wife every day on Skype. We talk about everything using webcams and texts, as if I'm right there with her. Last week she took her iPhone to my kid's baseball game and turned on the webcam. I watched the whole game. It was awesome. I even went to ice cream with the family afterward, even though I'm thousands of miles away.

—Ray, thirty-seven, Army ranger

1

Statistics tell us that there are well over two billion Internet users world-wide.[1] Asia leads the way with more than a billion users. The United States has over 273 million users (more than three-quarters of the population). The least technologically developed continent, Africa, has just over 167 million Internet users, which is about 15 percent of that continent's population. However, the number of African users is rapidly growing, increasing by 3,600 percent since the year 2000. Overall, more than one-third of the world's population is online, and that percentage increases daily.

For those actively involved in life online, it is difficult to fathom human existence before the Internet. If you travel a lot for work or pleasure you are undoubtedly grateful that smartphones, webcams, and social media provide easy and inexpensive ways for you to keep in touch with family, friends, coworkers, and the world at large. Digital technology is also incredibly useful if you're in or developing a long-term, long-distance relationship, as texting and webcams allow you to interact as often as you'd like and in many of the same ways as when you're in the same room. Even if you're single, digital technology is a boon, allowing you to seek partners and e-date—even to have virtual sex—with less focus than ever on who lives or works where. Today people residing in different countries or even on different continents can realistically meet and fall in love, with the vast majority of their relationship facilitated by digital devices.

It's not all about romance, either. Today, instantaneous access to breaking news and other current information is virtually unlimited. Online discussion groups allow free exchange of ideas and support for thousands of hobbies, interests, and personal concerns. People with chronic illnesses can greet their doctor with computer printouts detailing the latest treatments for their specific medical problem. And, perhaps most important of all, digital interconnectivity lets us witness and even participate in historic events from far away. In short, more people have more access to more "life" than ever before. And they can find all of it easily, instantly, and usually for free.

QUICKENING THE PACE

Have you ever watched a classic movie or read a nineteenth-century novel and been disappointed at the molasses-slow pace? Did you know that current television programs and movies have more and shorter scenes than those made just a few years ago? Rapid scene changes have become our entertainment norm. Inexorably, and without being aware of it, we have grown accustomed to a much faster pace in books, on television, and on the silver screen. And thanks to the Internet and other forms of digital technology, this quickening pace has spilled over into nearly every facet of our existence. These days we just don't have the time or the patience to wait for much of anything. We want what we want and we want it right now, and digital technology obliges.

A hundred years ago the tempo of life was very different. A visit to a relative who lived ten miles away was a major trip. It required an entire weekend to get there, visit, and return. Today that's a fifteen minute drive. A one week turnaround in response to a letter was once considered quick. Today, emails and texts arrive instantly and can be responded to in seconds. It used to be that major news events took many days to fully reach the public. For instance, after the "unsinkable" *Titanic* collided with an iceberg and sank in the north Atlantic on April 15, 1912, it was several days before most people in the United States were aware of the tragedy. In contrast, almost a century later, on January 15, 2009, when U.S. Airways flight 1549 crash landed in the Hudson River, much of the world watched the rescue of passengers either online or on television *as it happened*.

THE PORNOGRAPHY EXPLOSION

Here is a basic fact about being human: as a species, we hunger for stimulation and gratification. These are actually part of the primary drives that ensure our species' survival. For instance, if we don't eat and have sex—both of which are usually highly stimulating and gratifying—we don't survive. As such, it is hardly surprising that digital technology, no matter its original purpose, is sometimes adapted and used for sexual gratification. One of the more obvious manifestations of this is online pornography.

Nobody knows exactly how much digital porn is out there or how often it is viewed. Reliable porn-related statistics are hard to find, primarily because the highly politicized nature of porn causes profoundly different sources to occasionally distort the real numbers. For example, the porn industry encourages the idea that it has billions of users worldwide. Such a perception helps to foster porn's legitimacy and to raise potential advertising revenues. At the same time, anti-porn activists also tend to quote inflated figures in an attempt to point out the "all-pervasive" nature of the pornography "problem."

What is crystal clear, regardless of distortions in the actual numbers, is that more people than ever can access an ever-expanding selection of sexually explicit materials in many ways. Furthermore, access to sexual content is no longer limited to private settings like a person's home or office. In short, pornography is now ubiquitous—accessed anytime, anywhere, with content ranging from seemingly benign traditional pinup-type photos to graphic videos depicting extreme sexual violence, degradation, and more. Yes, the digital porn explosion has caused many traditional porn outlets—adult bookstores peep shows, and XXX movie houses—to wane in popularity, but porn itself is more popular than ever.

ONLINE SEXUAL EXPLORATION

Pornography is hardly the lone digital sexual outlet. The anonymous, highly affordable access provided by computers, smartphones, and other digital devices has encouraged an almost infinite array of sexual exploration over the past two decades. Without the fear of personal discovery or the potential embarrassment of a face-to-face interaction, people are asking about, investigating, and exchanging information about sex and relationships in ways that weren't even possible a mere twenty-five years ago. Plus, people increasingly use digital technology as a way to meet and date, and to locate casual, anonymous, or paid-for sexual partners.

Many people also use the Internet to experience "virtual sex." This idea is not exactly new. In fact, it has long been a staple of science fiction. One amusing cinematic example occurs in the 1973 movie *Sleeper*, starring

Woody Allen and Diane Keaton. In the movie, the "orgasmatron," a telephone booth-like contraption, helps users become sexually aroused by stimulating their brains in an intensely sexual way. Allen actually confirmed the scientific feasibility of this idea prior to making the film, so it's not surprising to learn about the existence of a real orgasmatron that was discovered serendipitously in trials for a potential spinal cord stimulator. The device apparently works rather well, but it costs quite a bit of money and requires the surgical insertion of electrodes near the spine. Needless to say, it is not widely used for pleasurable purposes.

A number of less intrusive sexual devices, however, are in widespread use. For instance, RealTouch has created a "teledildonic" male masturbation device that synchronizes genital simulation in real time with whatever online porn is being viewed. Working in tandem with the activities occurring onscreen, the device warms itself up, lubricates, pulses, and grips. The process can also be engaged in with a live person—a loved one, a webcam performer, even a random stranger—who at their end stimulates a sensor-covered rod that transmits live signals across the digital universe to the receiving RealTouch device. In other words, people can give and receive virtual masturbation and oral sex via the Internet. Other digitally driven devices can be used to pleasure women in a similar fashion. And more sophisticated "stuff" is on its way.

There are also a wide variety of virtual sex games accessible on pretty much any digital device. In these adult-oriented games, participants create customized fantasy avatars (animated figures of themselves or others) and then use those avatars to participate in interactive online sexcapades. At least one company is working to make its 3D sex games compatible with the Xbox Kinect so users can "touch" the avatars. As of now, most virtual sex games target heterosexual males, but there are also games for gay men, straight women, lesbians, bisexuals, and the fetish/kink community. Some games allow users to essentially produce their own porn—choosing erotic scenarios, camera angles, musical scores, oversized body parts, you name it. Whatever it is that turns you on, you can make it happen right now online.

Also evolving is onscreen eye-tracking technology, where tiny monitors track a user's eye movements as he or she scrolls through, reads, and otherwise views webpages and documents. Ostensibly this technology is intended for communications, game playing, and as a way for handicapped people to interact with technology and the world at large. For instance, when a user is reading a document and his or her eyes show that he or she has reached the bottom of the page, the device will bring up the next page. Eye tracking also lets digital devices glean information about users by tracking how many nanoseconds a person's gaze lingers on one part of a screen versus another. Eventually, using this technology, pornographers will be able to figure out what it is that most profoundly arouses each person, automatically using that information to bring up images and videos that mirror the user's deepest desires. In fact, it won't even matter if the person is consciously aware of his or her arousal patterns, because the digital device will know.

Then we have the Muse and the iBrain—headband-like devices that measure intra-skull electrical activity, helping people to act through brainwaves alone. In time, using brain readers, people will be able to control any electronic device solely by thought. This means that a quadriplegic could potentially walk again using mechanical legs controlled by information sent from the headband. Sexually, of course, the possibilities are endless. With a headband and a willing partner, those separated by distance because of work or school (or sheer laziness) will be able to merely think about stimulating their special someone and, voilà, using any number of teledildonic devices, those thoughts may become action.

Technology doesn't stop there, either. The KissPhone allows you to receive digital kisses, ostensibly from your wife, boyfriend, or grandmother. With KissPhones, the person on one end of the digital connection kisses his or her phone, and that device measures lip pressure, temperature, movement, and so on, and then transmits that information to the KissPhone at the other end, which reconstructs the kiss. It's hardly a leap to envision a digitally accessed bank of movie star and porn performer kisses—and more—all available for a price.

If that's not enough to rattle your chain, very soon people will be able to experience their entire partner's body, not just his or her lips, in a tech-bed, as sheets and sleepwear are being designed with special fibers that produce sensory responses, allowing people to "feel" the sensations of partner intimacy and sex no matter how far away the other person might be. And should you become less aroused by the physical reality of your long-term partner's looks, no problem, as developers are hard at work creating contact lenses that change the way that person looks to the viewer.

And what about robots? Already we have robots programmed to wash your hair, serve you tea, and mow your lawn. How much longer will it be before Rosie (the talking, emoting robotic maid from the cartoon *The Jetsons*) is built for real? And what happens when Rosie's manufacturer decides she needs to look like a life-sized Barbie doll, complete with pliable breasts and a synthetic vagina? And if Rosie the Robot who looks like Barbie is personality programmed to act as if she adores you, then what? Could wedding bells be very far behind?

Consider the 2013 movie *Her*, the tale of Theodore, a lonely man in the final stages of a bitter divorce. Feeling down, he treats himself to the new OS1, the world's first artificially intelligent operating system. Almost immediately, he finds himself enjoying the company and personality of Samantha, the voice behind his OS1, and he begins interacting with her on a personal level. Before he knows it, he and Samantha have fallen "in love." As absurd as this plotline sounds, the love story is incredibly compelling and feels quite real to the viewer. And a real world version of this is likely closer than you may think.

Scientist David Levy, an internationally recognized expert on artificial intelligence, predicts that by 2050 technology will have progressed to the point where "humans will fall in love with robots, humans will marry robots, and humans will have sex with robots, all as 'normal' extensions of our feelings of love and sexual desire."[2] And Levy is hardly alone in his belief that humans can and soon will interact on a very real emotional level with artificial life forms. In fact, Japanese researchers have already shown that well-programmed therapy robots can get antisocial children to smile and to interact positively with both other children and their caregivers.[3] So is falling in love with a sexually and emotionally attractive robot really so far-fetched? We think not.

BACK TO CURRENT REALITY

Certainly most digital technologies are not intended for sexual purposes. Yes, many are adapted for sex, but for the most part people rely on digital technology to communicate, to learn, to be entertained, to purchase goods, and to interact in healthy nonsexual ways. Unfortunately, some people can and do get lost in the endless pleasure that digital sexnologies can provide, over time losing control and becoming addicted.

CHAPTER ONE

SEX, TECH,
AND ADDICTION

In those rare times lately when I sit back and take stock of myself, I can see that I'm spending hour after hour, evenings and weekends, just sitting around staring at porn. Instead of actually having "a life," I've lost precious hours, days, weeks, months, and even years to isolation and loneliness. Most days I can't wait for work to end so I can get home to my porn collection. Whoever says this problem doesn't exist should try walking in my shoes for a few days.

—Jack, forty-four, cable TV installer

I don't know what it is to have a real relationship because all I've ever experienced is webcam hookups and porn.

—Kate, twenty-two, college student

My fiancée is cheating, but she won't admit it. Over the past six months she has "friended" a bunch of men on Facebook, and her phone is loaded with sexts that she sent to random guys. She says she's not doing anything wrong because she never meets any of them in-person and it's just a game for her. But it doesn't feel that way to me. I don't know what to do.

—Franklin, thirty-one, investment banker

WHAT IS SEXUAL ADDICTION?

For the most part, the criteria for sexual addiction are similar to any other addiction, including substance addictions:

1. Ongoing obsession/preoccupation with the drug/behavior of choice
2. Loss of control over use (inability to stop)
3. Continuation despite directly related negative life consequences

Today most people have some sense of what it might be like to have an addiction to alcohol or drugs, as they've either experienced it themselves or seen it in a friend or family member (or at least on TV). However, many folks have difficulty wrapping their heads around the concept of a behavioral addiction. This is especially true when the activity is a natural and even necessary part of life, as is the case with eating and being sexual.

The main difference between healthy sex (or healthy eating) and addictive sex (or addictive eating) is that addicts engage in the behavior compulsively as a way to "emotionally numb out" and "escape," and they continue to do so even as their clearly out-of-control behavior is creating significant problems in their lives—relationship issues, trouble at work or in school, declining physical and/or emotional health, financial turmoil, loss of interest in previously enjoyable activities, legal issues, family problems, and more. In essence, if a person is compulsively and persistently using sexual fantasy, sexual content, and sexual activity as a means of self-soothing or dissociating from stressful emotions or underlying psychological conditions (early-life trauma, depression/anxiety, attachment deficits, social deficits, or low self-esteem), that person is most likely a sex addict.

HOW TECHNOLOGY FEEDS SEXUAL ADDICTION

The more deeply one looks into the world of digital technology, the more obvious it becomes that anyone who is looking online for highly arousing sexual content and willing sexual partners both can and will find an unending supply. On the one hand, this is great, as the backyard dating and mating pond of yesteryear has now become a big giant ocean. On the other hand, this unlimited access can be incredibly problematic for people predisposed to addiction. In truth, digital sexual activities are a problem-free source of temporary pleasure and amusement for most people. However, those who are vulnerable to addiction can easily find themselves lost in an escalating, obsessive, online quest for "more, different, and better."

Research conducted in the 1980s (pre-Internet) suggested that 3 to 5 percent of the U.S. adult population struggled with addictive sexual behaviors. Mostly these folks were adult men hooked on video porn, affairs, prostitution, old-fashioned phone sex, and similar activities. In that era, little to no research was then done on women. Not surprisingly, that percentage jumped significantly with the arrival of home computers and the Internet. A well-known study conducted in the late 1990s was the first to confirm this. This groundbreaking Stanford University survey looked at the behavior of more than 9,000 Internet users, finding that 8.5 percent qualified as sexually addicted.[1] So basically the study found that access to the Internet approximately doubled the propensity for sexual addiction.

People in the Stanford study were considered to have a problem with addictive sex under the following circumstances:

- They described feeling "obsessed" or "driven" by online sexuality, as if it had become a "life priority."
- They'd made repeated, unsuccessful attempts to decrease or eliminate their online sexual activities.
- They continued going online for sex despite clearly related poor academic or job performance, relationship difficulties, job loss, sexual harassment lawsuits, arrests, failed relationships, or other adverse consequences.

Interestingly, a follow-up analysis revealed that only about 1 percent of the people who qualified as sex addicts reported a pre-Internet history of compulsive sexual activity. In other words, only a few of those who were identified as sexually addicted had problems with addictive sexual behaviors before the Internet came along. For them, the Internet simply became another means of accessing their long-standing obsession. For the rest, digital technology either led to or greatly facilitated the development of their addictive sexual behavior.

More recent studies indicate this "tech facilitates sex addiction" trend reinforces itself with each new development in digital technology. And the problem is no longer limited to adult men. Thanks to digital technology, the incidence of sexual addiction is also rising among women and adolescents of both genders. There is no doubt that these changes are directly related to the easy, affordable, and mostly anonymous access to pornography, willing sexual partners, and other highly arousing sexual activities that the Internet and other forms of digital technology currently provide. In short, as digital technology has increased our access to potentially addictive sexuality, mental health professionals have seen a corresponding increase in the number and variety of people with compulsive porn use and cybersex addiction. It's just that simple.

THE LURE OF PORN

As clinicians treating sexual addiction and other sexual disorders are well aware, digital porn is the leader when it comes to tech-driven sexual addictions. This is hardly a surprise, given the current online porn explosion. And no, we're not exaggerating when we use the word "explosion." Current research tells us that 12 percent of today's websites are pornographic, 25 percent of search engine requests are porn-related, and 35 percent of all downloads are of sexualized imagery.[2] And all of these numbers are up significantly from just a few years ago, thanks primarily to the advent of user-generated (amateur) pornography. The result is that pornography of every ilk imaginable is now anonymously available to anyone, anytime, on practically any digital device, and more often than not it's free.

For most people who enjoy porn, the experience can provide a quick and convenient means to a pleasurable end. Typically, healthy people utilize pornography when an emotional or a close physical connection is either not available or not desired, or when simply seeking self-pleasure. Unfortunately, porn use can morph over time into an addiction, ultimately leading to shame, secrecy, compartmentalization, humiliation, and a wide variety of other negative life consequences.

Generally speaking, porn addiction occurs when someone loses control over whether they will view and use pornography, the amount of time they will spend looking at pornography, and the types of pornography they will use. Research suggests that porn addicts typically spend at least eleven hours per week engaging with digital porn.[3] Often they spend double or even triple that amount. The following is Steve's story.

I work nine to five as an insurance claims adjustor. I wake up early every morning to masturbate—something I started in my early teens. Usually I grab my laptop while I'm still in bed, open up a porn site, and masturbate to videos of women defiling or abusing themselves in some way. I feel bad about being turned on by stuff that seems degrading to women, but I can't help myself. I didn't always look at that stuff—I actually thought it was disgusting—but now I can't seem to stay away from it.

Sometimes I use my smartphone to watch porn while I'm in the car. I like watching porn in the car more than anywhere else because it's exciting and forbidden, and it takes my mind off of traffic and everything else that bothers me about my life. And, as part of my job, I'm on the road a lot—so I watch porn quite a bit. I've gotten tickets for driving erratically because of this, but I've always managed to switch the phone off before a police officer or anyone else can catch me in the act.

In the evenings I have "dinner and a show," which means pizza or takeout Chinese food and several hours of porn beamed wirelessly from my laptop to the forty-six-inch flat-screen in my living room. My goal is always to find that one perfect video that I haven't seen before. Usually even a so-so new video is better than a really good one I've seen a few times. On an average day, I can easily lose three or four hours to

masturbation and porn. And sadly, even to me, on an average day—apart from interactions related to my work and purchasing food or gasoline—I don't talk to or interact with a single human being.
                                        —Steve, twenty-nine, insurance claims adjustor

Steve's experience is not unusual for a self-reported porn addict for the following reasons:

- His seemingly unending involvement with pornography prevents him from engaging in any genuinely intimate, real world interaction.
- He is constantly searching for his next sexual "high," which is brought on by the intensity of each new video or simply the fantasy of what each new video might bring.
- His porn use has escalated to the point that he is now aroused by sexual content that he does not feel good about watching.
- He justifies his behavior with lame excuses like "I just can't help myself."
- His experience is framed around the fantasy of future sex such as searching for the perfect new video rather than sex itself.

THE GREAT PORN DEBATE

Currently there is panic about young males and their nearly ubiquitous use of Internet porn. When Canadian researcher Simon Lajeunesse attempted to perform research into the effects of porn on young males, he was stymied in his efforts because he couldn't find any college-aged males who weren't porn users; and without a control group, there was no way for him to make comparisons. Countless parents are worried about or horrified by their sons' fascination with and use of Internet porn. And more than a few people are talking openly about the negative effects of porn use on young males.

In his book, *The Demise of Guys: Why Boys are Struggling and What We Can Do About It*, Phillip Zimbardo writes, "From the earliest ages, guys are seduced into excessive and mostly isolated viewing and involvement with...

pornography."[4] Zimbardo then asserts that thanks to all of this porn consumption young males' brains are being rewired to demand unrealistic levels of novelty, stimulation, and excitement, and as a result they are becoming out of sync with real world relationships. Gary Wilson, creator and moderator of the popular yourbrainonporn.com website, also asserts that young male porn users may experience a loss of interest in real world intimacy, plus a variety of other issues typically associated with compulsive sexuality.[5]

On Wilson's website these fears are backed up with first-person postings by young men who've written into the site, detailing their experiences with porn usage saying things like:

- I started watching porn around the age of 10 and fapping (masturbating) around the age of 14. It got up to 2 to 3 times a day for the last four years, until I decided to quit. I had many reasons for starting nofap (abstinence from masturbation)—girls, anxiety, depression, and I couldn't figure out why I felt so dead inside.
- I had weird fetishes and I couldn't stay aroused or erect during sex or even masturbation.
- What was worse than the PIED [Porn-Induced Erectile Dysfunction] was the desensitization to the world. I found it hard to enjoy anything at all.

Clearly the young men posting their stories on the website have experienced consequences—not only emotional but physical—related to their porn use. The questions that can't be answered without further investigation are whether these guys are actually addicted to porn or just casual/heavy users, and whether all young males who regularly access porn are being similarly affected. In reality, there is very little research on the topic, so we don't know for certain what online porn is doing to the majority of young males who are looking at it. However, we do know they are looking at very early ages (for boys, the average age of first exposure to Internet porn is eleven[6]), and we know that *some* boys are being negatively affected.

In all likelihood, the majority of boys who look at porn will do so without serious problems, just as most boys who try alcohol will do so without ever becoming alcoholic. However, kids who are vulnerable to addiction thanks to either genetics or difficult life circumstance (or both) are definitely at risk for porn and cybersex addiction, just as they are at risk for developing alcoholism or drug addiction if they start experimenting with potentially addictive substances.

The following is an incomplete listing of factors that increase a young person's vulnerability to addictions of all stripes:

- Prior addiction in a family member
- History of neglect
- History of emotional, physical, or sexual abuse
- Social anxiety
- Depression
- Attention deficit disorder (ADD)
- Obsessive compulsive disorder (OCD)
- History of self-harm behaviors (cutting, burning, etc.)
- Disordered eating (binging and purging, anorexia, etc.)
- Falling anywhere on the Asperger's spectrum
- Learning disabilities
- Impulsivity toward high risk or intensity-driven behaviors

Of course, addiction is not just about vulnerability factors. Even people without genetic predispositions toward addiction and/or family-of-origin issues can be at risk—especially if they start in with a pleasure-inducing substance or behavior early in life. Research proves this rather conclusively with alcoholism and drug addiction, with numerous studies showing that the earlier the age of first exposure to these substances and the more frequent the use, the higher the likelihood of addiction.[7]

It seems reasonable to assume that the same is probably true with porn, although there is not currently any research to this effect, nor is there likely to be any such research in the near future. After all, as Gary Wilson writes,

"First, who can find porn virgins of a suitable age [to use as a control group]? Second, who deliberately wants to expose kids to super-stimulating erotic videos to see what happens in their brains, or how it alters their sexual response over time?"[8] This means that the only research we can realistically hope for is after-the-fact surveys of self-identified adult porn addicts, asking about when they were first exposed to digital porn, how much they used, and why. And even that research is "down the road" several years because the Internet porn explosion is such a new phenomenon.

EVERYTHING ELSE UNDER THE SUN

Porn, of course, is merely the tip of the sexnology (technology used to generate or enhance sexual pleasure) iceberg. These days it is entirely possible to meet a potential sex partner using a smartphone hookup app, to flirt with that person via texts and sexts, to be sexual with that person via webcam and teledildonic devices, and then to brag about the encounter by posting on some form of social media. And the person with whom you've had this torrid sexual fling has never even been in the same room as you because the entire interaction has occurred online.

As you can see, digital sexual activity extends well beyond the bounds of pornography.

> *I started downloading and masturbating to porn and chatting with women I met online when I was a teenager. Eventually this advanced to nightly participation in video chats and mutual masturbation via webcam. A few years ago, when I got a smartphone, I took my show on the road, sexting my regular online partners and seeking out new ones. Thanks to a couple of hookup apps, I was able to meet several women in my hometown. Suddenly, despite having no previous history of in-the-flesh adultery, I found myself meeting nearby women for casual sex. I sought help only when my wife found out about my behavior and threatened to leave me.*

> *Looking back, I am amazed by the immense amount of time and energy I put into sexual activity. As a teen, it interfered with my*

schoolwork. My homework either didn't get done or was done poorly because I was in a rush to get online. As an adult, it created emotional distance, frustration, and impatience in dating relationships and later with my wife and children, and it took up work time and office resources. Plus, waiting until my wife went to sleep and then staying up on the computer until two or three in the morning left me, more often than not, tired, exhausted, depressed, and physically unwell. Our marital sex life became practically nonexistent, and I watched my wife blame herself, thinking she was no longer attractive. Despite all the craziness, I still think about getting back online nearly every day.

—Hank, forty-two, systems analyst

Here are some of the most common engaged-in digital sexual activities:

- Joining sexual membership communities that serve various interests
- Posting personal profiles (dating and/or sex ads), and hooking up with other people either online or IRL (in real life)
- Meeting people with similar sexual interests—such as fetishes, spouses looking to cheat, or older people looking for romance—via chat rooms, websites, and smartphone apps
- Viewing and downloading porn photos or videos from people, commercial porn sites, newsgroups, or file transfer protocol (FTP) sites
- Exchanging texts, emails, and photos with others for the purpose of sexual/romantic fantasy, possibly leading to solo masturbation, mutual masturbation via webcam, or in-person sexual encounters
- Using prostitute, escort, and sexual massage websites and apps
- Buying, selling, or otherwise exchanging traditional sex-industry products such as magazines, videos, and sex toys
- Simultaneous mutual sexual activity in private chat rooms—writing back and forth while masturbating, or masturbating on video chat
- Viewing, via webcam, staged sexual acts in real time
- Using apps to find casual and/or anonymous sexual hookups
- Cruising social media or dating sites to view intimate photos or locate potential sexual partners

- Sexting (sending sexual texts and images) via smartphones as a way to flirt with an existing partner or a new acquaintance, or even just for the sexual thrill of it
- Using teledildonic masturbatory devices that warm, lubricate, pulse, and grip in tandem with sexual activities taking place onscreen such as porn videos or even live performances
- Playing virtual sex games that allow users to create customized fantasy avatars that are then used to participate in interactive online sexcapades

Given the amount and variety of currently available digital sexual activities, it is easy to see why sex addiction is on the rise.

The "Triple-A Engine"

Nearly all modern day sex addicts have fallen victim to the Internet's Triple-A Engine[9] of accessibility, affordability, and anonymity. To understand how the Triple-A Engine works, consider the following stories about porn use and casual sex thirty years ago versus today.

Porn in 1985: Joe, a resident of Boston, wanted to look at porn one day, so he got up, got dressed, and rode the train for nearly half an hour to the city's infamous "Combat Zone," where he knew about an adult bookstore. There he spent nearly $100 on a small pile of magazines filled with grainy imagery. For Joe, that was quite a lot of money—more than he could really afford. Plus, he spent the entire trip watching over his shoulder hoping to not be seen by a friend, neighbor or someone from his church. Over the course of the next few weeks Joe enjoyed looking at and masturbating to the pornography, but as the imagery became increasingly familiar, he lost interest. Within a month he was back on the train, surreptitiously headed back to the Combat Zone, ready to once again spend money he didn't really have on a new batch of pornography.

Porn in 2015: Joe picked up his smartphone on his nightstand and uttered the words, "show me some porn." No train ride, no $100 outlay, and no boredom with the imagery because the Internet provides an endless and ever-changing supply. No muss, no fuss, just the porn, thank you very much.

Seeking a one night stand in 1985: Amy, an unmarried resident of Minneapolis, was feeling lonely one evening. Hoping to meet Mr. Right (or at least Mr. Right Now) she showered, styled her hair, put on makeup, spritzed herself with perfume, and slipped into her slinky black dress. Then she walked downstairs from her second floor apartment into the freezing cold Minnesota winter, hailed a cab, and took an expensive ride to a singles bar on the other side of town (not wanting any of her friends or neighbors to see her and figure out what she was up to). At the club she bought herself a couple of overpriced drinks and waited for a decent looking man to display interest in her. Several men offered to buy her a drink, but none of them were her "type." Eventually, dejected and depressed, she left the bar and took the long cab ride home.

Seeking a one night stand in 2015: Amy was feeling lonely one evening. She put some popcorn in the microwave while clicking on her Tinder smartphone app. While snacking in her bathrobe and slippers she noticed a cute guy right away. She swiped his profile to indicate interest, and before her microwave popcorn was gone she was sexting him. Twenty minutes later he arrived at her doorstep, happy to share popcorn, a movie, and a little bit more with her. No hours of preparation, no expensive cab ride or overpriced drinks, no parade of losers, no sore feet and ankles from standing around in high heels for three hours, and no disappointment at the end of the night.

The reality is that sexual content and contacts are now readily available to anyone at the touch of a digital button. Barriers that existed just a few decades ago no longer exist. You don't even need an actual computer. Laptops, tablets, e-readers, smartphones, gaming platforms, and numerous other devices will serve you nicely for tonight's sexual hookup. Nor do you need to be a techno-genius because digital devices, websites, and apps are incredibly user-friendly. Pornography and casual sexual connections can now be accessed anywhere, anytime, by anyone who's interested—with that interest typically fulfilled almost immediately. And this, of course, can be quite problematic for cybersex addicts.

Beyond the Triple-A Engine

As you can see, the accessibility, affordability, and anonymity of the Internet makes digital technology very attractive, particularly when it comes to sex. But there is more to the allure of digital technology than just the three A's.

Interactivity

The interactive nature of the Internet provides users with a profoundly different experience than other forms of entertainment. While television, film, radio, books, and magazines are static, the Internet is not. For instance, a porn magazine likely provides twenty or so pictures and that's it. With a porn DVD you get an hour or so of action and that's it. It doesn't matter if there's only one picture in the magazine or one scene in the video that turns you on. That's all you get. Period. If you're looking at porn online, however, you can sort and reshuffle images and sometimes, if you've got someone performing live via webcam, you might even be able to direct the action via live chat. The Internet provides you with control over whom and what you view in ways that other media simply cannot. Thanks to this interactivity, digital technology has the power to hold a person's interest far longer than any previous entertainment medium, especially when it comes to sexual content and romance.

> ### How Digital Technology
> ### Escalates Porn Addiction
>
> The idea that the Internet and related technologies can now provide an unending, ever-changing stream of sexualized imagery and experience is in great part what feeds porn addiction. Porn addiction, like other addictions, is driven as much by *anticipatory fantasy* as by the actual act (in this case, the act of masturbation and orgasm). Thanks to digital technology, porn now changes continually, allowing the cybersex addict to experience the "rush" of "the new" almost constantly.

Compactness/Portability

In the past, porn magazines ended up under the mattress, in piles the garage, or stacked in a closet. DVDs and VHS tapes also had to be stored—preferably in a place inaccessible to your kids or your spouse, not to mention visiting relatives and friends. For sexualized phone calls you needed someplace private, which was a real problem when all you had was a landline. For actual live sexual encounters, you needed a motel room or at least a car with a decent backseat. All these forms of sexual content and activity took up a lot of space making them hard to conceal. Today, digital sexual content and activity takes up no more space than the digital device you are using to access it. And if an unwanted visitor enters the room, a simple click can both end the connection and hide the evidence. A porn collection that would once have filled a three-car garage can now be stored on a USB flash drive no bigger than your thumb or in "the cloud." So in today's world, sexual acting out, even when excessive, is just a whole lot easier to manage, especially if your goal is to keep it secret.

Safety

Digital technology almost guarantees that you can go online and engage in digital sex *without the risk* of catching a sexually transmitted disease, getting arrested, or risking physical attack through robbery, assault, or rape. Plus, those who tend to be shy or socially withdrawn can lose their anxious inhibitions behind the safety shield provided by the mostly anonymous and non-intimate nature of online sexual life.

Online Community (The Good)

On the Internet, almost anyone can find a community to validate his or her personal interests and behaviors. People who are into cars can chat with others who are into cars. People with cancer can learn more about that disease, join support groups designed to help people with cancer, and gather information for potential treatments they can later discuss with their doctor. For lesbian, gay, bisexual, and transgender people—especially those who may have trouble or feel uncomfortable meeting like-minded others in the real world—computers can provide a supportive environment and a way of connecting. The same is true for people with unconventional or culturally frowned-upon sexual "lifestyles," such as those interested in cross-dressing or dominance-based sex.

Some Internet users with atypical or unconventional sexual interests such as BDSM, foot worship, and chubby chasing have formed "virtual communities" in support of their sexual interests. Nowadays, people whose patterns of sexual arousal previously marginalized them and caused them to hide or simply avoid/ignore their interest can readily find like-minded others who share their enthusiasm and are looking to engage in the sex that actually turns them on.

Online Community (The Bad)

The Internet is also, unfortunately, a place where people who have deviant or illegal sexual interests such as pedophilia or exhibitionism can exercise those interests. Prior to the Internet, many people flirted in fantasy with these various behaviors but were held back from acting out because of potential negative consequences, or they simply didn't have access to the people with whom they could have this type of sex. On the Internet they can find others who will support and encourage these interests, thereby lowering the boundary between fantasy and action. This has the strong potential to normalize harmful/illegal sexual behaviors for people who otherwise might never have indulged their interest, and the results can be catastrophic for both the person and their potential victims. In this respect, digital technology can sometimes drive not only sexual addiction but also sexual offending.

SEXUAL ADDICTION VS. SEXUAL OFFENDING

Sex addicts are men and women who engage compulsively in one or more sexual behaviors, continue these behaviors despite significant negative consequences, and spend a great deal of time thinking about, planning, and engaging in sexual activity. Over time, sex becomes the primary focus of their lives. A sex offender may have similar symptoms, but sex offenders differ in that they engage in sexual activities that violate the rights of others, break the law, or both.

- Sexual addiction takes place within the context of a solo sexual act or in a relationship with a *consenting* adult.
- Sexual offending involves *nonconsensual* forms of sex—sex with those who don't want it, sex with those who don't know it's happening (voyeurism), sex with those who are too young to consent (including viewing pornography featuring minors), sex with those who are mentally incapacitated and therefore can't consent, and sex by force.

Sex addiction may take away or diminish a person's health, self-esteem, marriage, or job, and may personally offend many people, but seeking or having a lot of indiscriminate sex is not the same as sexual offending. Although many spouses or partners of sex addicts worry that their children or families might be at risk because there is a sex addict in

the house, the reality is that few sex addicts are also sexual offenders. Their sexual choices and activities, while painful, problematic, and destructive to existing relationships, are typically consensual and legal.

ONLINE ADDICTIONS INVOLVE SOME PEOPLE BUT NOT MOST

Most people use digital technology in healthy ways that improve their lives in all facets, including their sexual lives. Only a small minority of people who go online, even for sexual purposes, struggle with their tech-driven behaviors. For those who do struggle, however, tech-driven sexuality can be every bit as problematic as an addiction to heroin, alcohol, gambling, binge eating, or cocaine. This painful reality will be examined further as this book progresses, starting in the next chapter, which is designed to help readers recognize the difference between simple pleasure seeking and sexual addiction.

CHAPTER TWO

PLEASURE SEEKER OR ADDICT? UNDERSTANDING THE DIFFERENCES

In my church we believe that any form of extramarital sex is a sin, including masturbating and looking at porn. But what am I supposed to do? I'm twenty-three and I'm not even dating, let alone married. I asked the minister about this, admitting to him that once or twice a month I go online to look at porn and masturbate. He looked at me with deep concern and suggested that I might be a sex addict. Am I? It seems to me that I'd need to be looking at porn a lot more than once or twice a month to be an addict. But I do believe that what I'm doing is morally wrong and I'd like to stop.

   —Paul, twenty-three, a student at a religious college

I'm single and I don't date, but I go online every night and look at porn. Sometimes I go to video chat sites and bounce around from person to person, looking for someone who will masturbate while I watch. I don't even care if it's a guy who's doing it, even though I'm straight. There's just something really intense about watching people get off. Usually, before I know it, I've been online for five or six hours. I keep telling myself I'll only go online for half an hour or so, but that never happens. I can't stop myself, and I never get enough sleep because of

*it. Now my grades are really dropping because I keep falling asleep in
class, and even when I'm awake in class I'm sneaking looks at porn on
my iPhone.*

—Rick, twenty-one, student

THE BRAIN WANTS WHAT THE BRAIN WANTS

Nearly everyone finds the gleaming dessert tray brought out at the end
of a good dining experience irresistible. Even if you've had enough to eat,
all that scrumptious pastry, moist cake, light and fluffy pie, and decadent
chocolate is bound to produce some longing and interest. Our bodies
respond to the anticipatory pleasure of dessert, even if we're not hungry.
And it's not just sweets that precipitate this reaction. Exposure to or fantasy
about sex, romance, spending, gambling, and more can all cause temporary
chemical changes in the brain, ignited by anticipatory interest and excitement. Our pupils dilate, our heart rates increase, our breathing grows faster
and shallower, and we may even perspire. In this process, we also become a
bit fuzzy intellectually, increasingly focused on the idea of pleasure. When
this occurs, a once definitive "no" turns into a "maybe" and eventually a
"yes." We quite literally lose our ability to follow through on intellectual
decisions.

This neurochemical change is actually a function of evolution and
"intelligent design." In other words, eating and being sexual are necessary
to survival of both the individual and the species because if we don't eat or
reproduce, we die out rather quickly. Thus, our brains are preprogrammed
to make us "experience pleasure" when we engage in these and similar life-
affirming activities. Essentially, when an "object of desire" comes within
reach of our senses, our brains release a flood of neurochemicals—primarily
dopamine but also serotonin, epinephrine (adrenaline), endorphins, and a
few others. These are the brain's mood-lifting and pain-regulating elements,
and it is this rapid alteration of brain chemistry—initiated through fantasy
and championed by the heightening of our five senses—that leaves us
feeling excited and pushed toward whatever it is that we see, smell, hear,
taste, touch, and increasingly desire.

We don't even have to actually engage with the activity or substance (i.e., dessert) to get excited. A mere lingering thought about a highly pleasurable previous experience begins this biologically based arousal process. We remember eating and savoring chocolate cake in the past, so when we see a similar offering in the present we want it. In fact, we crave it. This is the natural order of things.

Not surprisingly, then, everyone is at times tempted by a potentially pleasurable substance or activity. But we each have different levels of self-control that help us decide whether to move toward something enticing or stay away from it. Most of us are able to think before taking action, using past experience as a guide. People with strong impulse control can objectively decide if seeking a pleasurable experience has risks and, if so, whether the risks are worth it. For instance, someone starting a diet may consider, before diving in, "Is devouring that cake going to make me feel ashamed later and work against my goal of losing weight?" Similarly, in the arena of sex, healthy people may objectively ask, "Is having this flirtation or looking at these porn images going to affect my primary relationship in ways that I'll regret?"

The ability to pause and consider potential outcomes before taking an impulsive action is a key measure of emotional health. However, even a healthy person's ability to "just say no" can be compromised at times, depending on the strength of that person's desire and his or her current level of stress. If we get fired from a job or experience some other deep personal loss, some may decide to self-soothe with an extra martini, a cigarette (even though we quit smoking many years ago), a bag of chips, or sexual activity. Even good things can throw us off a bit. When we get a raise at work or experience the birth of our first grandchild, we may disregard some of our usual cautions in celebration. And during the holidays we may heartily overeat, justifying our behavior as part of that particular celebration.

Usually, though, it's the downside rather than the upside that sets us off. Typically, the more anxious, emotionally empty, and stressed out we become, the less likely we are to make our usual good decisions. And people who generally have trouble tolerating strong emotional reactions—those who tend toward impatience, impulsivity, and reactivity by nature—nearly always have an even harder time not reaching for immediate gratification without careful prior thought especially when temptation looms. If you're wondering whether you are just a bit impulsive or out of control, our next section will help you explore the range of cybersex use patterns from the casual user to the addict.

CASUAL VS. AT-RISK VS. ADDICTED USER

As you read through the following descriptions and characteristics, see if you recognize yourself or a loved one.

The Casual Cybersex User

Casual users of digital sexnology are men and women who find online pornography, virtual sexual experiences, and digital flirting to be sometimes fascinating and fun. They get involved in these pleasurable distractions occasionally, depending on their life circumstances, but not to extremes. Casual users typically find these activities to be an enjoyable distraction, a sporadic form of escape or relaxation that is ultimately not as satisfying or meaningful as more intimate connections.

The following statements are often true of casual cybersex users:

- Cybersex use is intermittent and occasional.
- Cybersex activity is driven by curiosity, novelty, education, or entertainment.
- Frequency of use is driven by life-stage events, such as more frequent use in late adolescence or when out of a relationship.
- Usage may temporarily increase after a personal loss or some other difficult life change, decreasing when life gets better.
- They do not have a history of profound early-life neglect or trauma, or extensive adult-life trauma.
- A strong sense of self gives them an inherent, consistent feeling of "being okay" and "good enough." When bad things happen, they

don't turn on themselves, and when good things happen, they can tolerate the pleasure and excitement.

- Their lives include stable, long-term friendships and a sense of belonging to a particular community.
- Their lives include recreation and play, and they willingly and easily allow themselves to relax.
- They are able to seek, find, and remain honest within committed, intimate partnerships.
- Their interest in porn and other online sexual experiences is not sustained over time because those experiences feel repetitive, two-dimensional, and unrealistic.
- They don't experience profound shame or self-hatred over these activities.

The At-Risk Cybersex User

At-risk users may go through periods of intense engagement with digital sexnology, sometimes using it as a distraction from emotional discomfort and other life problems. These users may have addiction-like periods of porn use and other tech-driven sexual activity, but they can (and usually do) limit or stop their behaviors when they start to experience adverse consequences or as their life circumstances improve. Characteristics of at-risk cybersex users may include the following:

- Keeping secrets—thereby sacrificing intimacy in exchange for "looking good," "being right," or "being accepted"
- A potential history of substance abuse for recreation, and related impulsive choices
- A potential history of abusing external stimulation (spending, gambling, sex, and other high-intensity behaviors) to achieve distraction from stress or extremes of mood
- Often reacting to emotional stressors with anger, sarcasm, blaming, and other forms of externalized feelings

- Having primary relationships that can be stormy, challenging, stifling, and/or lacking in empathy and healthy vulnerability
- Avoiding or being annoyed by people who express concern at the amount of time spent in online sexual activity
- Being narcissistic, not seeing their part in conflicts, and struggling to understand others' frustrations
- Being sensitive, taking things personally

While not necessarily addicted or even compulsive about their cybersex activities, at-risk users can at times look a lot like sex addicts—hiding the nature and extent of their sexual/romantic behaviors, ignoring both actual and potential consequences, and escalating the nature and extent of their use. What differentiates at-risk users from sex addicts is *at-risk users can stop their sexual behaviors on their own* and sex addicts cannot. The at-risk user, in essence, retains control and choice over whether he or she engages in cybersex. By definition, addicts have lost this ability to choose.

The Addicted Cybersex User

In today's world, sex addicts are people who compulsively use digital technology to engage in sexual fantasy and behaviors regardless of the potential consequences to themselves and others. Yes, there are still a few sex addicts who don't rely on digital technology to facilitate their sexual acting out, but these folks are few and far between. Though many sex addicts externally exude confidence and self-worth, this is usually an emotional mask that covers underlying issues with low self-esteem, shame, anxiety, depression, and poor self-worth. Even when they are incredibly successful on the outside, sex addicts feel empty within. And they repeatedly turn to digitally driven sexual fantasy and connections to temporarily fill that emotional void. Sadly, they are unable to stop their problematic behaviors on their own, even when they experience negative consequences or a desire for change.

Characteristics of sexually addicted users may include the following:

- Living a double life—keeping significant information about sexual activity hidden from family and others
- A history of or current problems with anxiety, depression, and related emotional challenges
- A history of substance abuse, eating disorders, and other compulsive, impulsive, or addictive behaviors
- A history of childhood abuse, trauma, or neglect, which, without therapy, they might not acknowledge, accept emotionally, or fully understand
- A history of profound early-life family dysfunction, including violence, neglect, addiction, or mental illness
- Lifelong fears of being unwanted or abandoned if they are ever fully honest and fully known to intimate friends and partners
- Lack of empathy toward those directly and indirectly affected by the addict's sexual behavior
- Using porn, casual sex, or masturbation to replace deeply intimate personal relationships and peer support
- A history of intimacy problems and relationship concerns— breaking commitments, harming others, leaving relationships for no apparent reason
- A history of profound, unresolved adult trauma (war, physical violence, rape, etc.)
- A pattern of leaving or not knowing how to maintain relationships when the initial excitement of a new person has worn off
- A pattern of being superficially engaged but emotionally distant in friendships and other relationships
- Lack of empathy toward those directly and/or indirectly affected by the addict's sexual behavior (narcissism)
- Using porn, casual sex, and/or masturbation to replace or avoid deeply intimate personal relationships and peer support

UNDERSTANDING CYBERSEX ADDICTS

People who become addicted to using the intensity of sexual fantasy and activity for emotional distraction and self-soothing are essentially drug addicts, but instead of using something obtained externally to numb out and escape such as pills or alcohol, they have learned to exploit their internal pleasure-producing processes—that is, their own neurochemistry. Over time, their life priorities shift from family, work, recreation, and community to the repetitive pursuit of pleasurable stimulation via sexual content and behavior. Other people and healthy life experiences become secondary to their search for the emotional high provided by sexual fantasy, arousal, and activity. The self-induced neurochemical stimulation provided by hours of looking at porn, playing virtual sex games, being sexual on webcams, and cruising for sexual or romantic partners on dating sites, social media, and apps becomes their "drug of choice."

Cybersex addicts continue their problematic behaviors despite feeling bad about themselves and damaging their life goals and personal relationships. Sometimes they attempt to control their problem by switching from one behavior to another. For example, a cybersex addict may move from compulsive porn use to seeking live partners via smartphone apps. Unfortunately, switching types of sexual activity does not solve the problem. This is a bit like an alcoholic who, having had too many problems when drinking vodka, switches to wine. He has not stopped drinking; he has merely found a different way of achieving the same high. People in recovery sometimes call this "rearranging the deck chairs on the *Titanic*." The view may be a little different, but the ship is still sinking.

As noted previously, sexual addiction is more about the anticipation of sex than actual sexual activity. Even before sitting down to search for online porn or to seek out potential sex partners, sex addicts are "high," meaning the anticipation of the sexual experience leaves them both emotionally aroused and distracted. If you struggle with this concept, consider the example of a drug addict who, cash in hand, has finally found a source for the drugs he or she so desperately desires. While on the way to the ATM, withdrawing money, and driving to the dealer's house, isn't this person "high" already? After all, his or her thinking is impaired and he or she is already making bad decisions. And the closer the addict gets to actually using the drugs, the harder the heart pounds, the clammier the hands feel, and the less informed the person's thinking becomes. Yet, at this point, there are no drugs in the addict's system.

Cybersex addiction operates in much the same way. Sex addicts find as much intensity, excitement, and distraction in the search for their next sexual thrill as in the sex act itself. Intense sexual fantasies pull sex addicts into an emotional state that renders them relatively unable to make better choices or to consider how their behaviors might affect others. This is the same type of emotional state that compulsive gamblers feel when sitting at a craps table with their kid's college fund stacked in chips in front of them. They know they shouldn't play with that money, but what if the next hand brings that big win, or the hand after that, or the hand after that…. Such is the face of behavioral addictions.

Sex addicts in treatment often refer to this intense emotional state as being in "the trance" or "the bubble." They can spend hours, sometimes even days, in this elevated condition, high on the goal or idea of sex without engaging in any actual sexual act. Yet. So for addicts—substance abusers and behavioral addicts alike—the fantasies and rituals that precede the using/acting out behaviors are every bit as compelling and addictive as the actual drug or behaviors, perhaps more so. Locked into fantasy and sexual obsession, the cybersex addict's emotionally charged neurochemical high is maintained and/or increased by the ongoing searching, watching, downloading, chatting, texting, sexting, and other fantasy-based sexual behaviors. Every new picture, video, game, or person sends messages to the addict's brain to release more dopamine, helping the addict to maintain the desired level of distraction and arousal. Like addicted gamblers waiting with bated breath for the next card to be dealt, cybersex addicts keep themselves in a constant state of excitement through all of their searching, anticipating, and fantasizing.

The simple reality of cybersexual addiction is that addicts can spend hours on end feeling intense emotional arousal without becoming physically aroused, masturbating, or having an orgasm. Their obsessive search for and fantasy about finding the perfect image, video, or sexual partner can keep them distracted and disengaged from stressful priorities, relationships, and life commitments every bit as effectively as heroin, cocaine, or any other mood-altering substance.

Sometimes the addict's spouse or partner confronts the addict: "What about me and our relationship? Don't you know how your looking at porn every night affects us? I thought you loved me!" Sadly, the reality for cybersex addicts is that during their sexual fantasies they are so focused on the intensity of what they are doing that they literally aren't able to think about much else. Porn addicts can tap away at computers, laptops, tablets, and smartphones for hours or even days, often saying to themselves, "I'll stop in ten minutes," or, "I'll stop for dinner," or, "I'll stop when I have to put the kids to bed." Meanwhile, ten minutes comes and goes, dinner gets cold, and frustrated loved ones give up and go to bed alone.

Although the final outcome of sexual acting out for most cybersex addicts is orgasm, that is not the actual goal. For addicts, the real goal is the emotional distraction provided by all the looking, cruising, contacting, and downloading—and none of that has anything to do with orgasm. In fact, once orgasm occurs, the "bubble" pops and reality floods back in. At that point, the addict is reminded of the late hour, promises made and broken, and yet another night with not enough sleep.

Am I a Cybersex Addict?

The use of digital technology for sexual purposes ranges from casual to addictive. We suggest you take the following quiz to see if you have crossed the line between casual use and addictive use.

CYBERSEX ADDICTION SCREENING TEST

The following Cybersex Addiction Screening Test (CAST-R) is designed to assist in the assessment of tech-driven compulsive and/or addictive sexual behavior. The test provides a profile of responses that can help to identify men and women with tech-driven sexual addiction disorders.

Instructions

Check each "yes" or "no" response as appropriate, and then tabulate your "yes" responses.

1. Do you find yourself spending increasing amounts of time online (including mobile devices) looking at porn and/or engaging in sexual or romantic fantasy, even when you have other things to accomplish that you are putting aside to be sexual?
   ☐ YES   ☐ NO

2. Have you promised yourself that you will stop viewing or using certain sexual websites or apps only to find yourself back there again anyway?
   ☐ YES   ☐ NO

3. Do you find yourself involved in hidden romantic or sexual affairs, either online or in-person?
   ☐ YES   ☐ NO

4. Do you extensively collect pornography or sexual contacts, store images and videos, romantic emails, and texts related to past and present acting out partners and activities in your computer or elsewhere?
   ☐ YES   ☐ NO

5. Do you find yourself habitually going online to see who might be available for sex and/or romance even when you don't have time or it was not your clear intention to do so?
   ☐ YES   ☐ NO

6. Have you had negative consequences at work, in school, in relationships, or in other important areas of your life related to your online porn use or other digitally driven sexual activity?
    ☐ YES   ☐ NO

7. Has your focus on porn use and/or a digital sexual life led to a decreased focus on friends, family, faith-based, and/or recreational activities?
    ☐ YES   ☐ NO

8. Has your digital sexual behavior caused you to lose anything or anyone important to you (career, school, relationships, finances, self-esteem, health, etc.)?
    ☐ YES   ☐ NO

9. Do you lie or keep secrets from those close to you about your involvement with online porn, the type of porn you view, or other digital sexual activities?
    ☐ YES   ☐ NO

10. Have you found yourself covering up or hiding your porn use or other digitally driven sexual activity so that a spouse, coworker, or family member won't discover it?
    ☐ YES   ☐ NO

11. If in a committed relationship, would your partner/spouse say that your porn use and/or other digitally driven sexual activity violates the underlying agreements surrounding your relationship (if he or she knew everything)?
    ☐ YES   ☐ NO

12. Do you feel that your involvement with online porn and digitally driven sexual activity is interfering with other personal goals like developing relationships, healthy intimacy, and/or a family/community life?
    ☐ YES   ☐ NO

13. Have you found yourself viewing sexual material or engaging in sexual activity that is illegal?
    ☐ YES   ☐ NO

14. Have you heard complaints and concern from family or friends about the amount of time you spend online looking at porn or the type of porn you view?
    ☐ YES   ☐ NO

15. Do you become defensive, angry, or extremely ashamed when asked to look at, give up, or reduce your porn use or your other online sexual involvements?
    ☐ YES   ☐ NO

Total YES answers _____

SCORING:

1 or 2 "yes" answers: You are likely a "casual" user of digital sexual technology.

3 or 4 "yes" answers: You are probably an "at-risk" user of digital sexual technology. It is important that you talk to others, as a way to monitor potential problems, about your engagement with digital sexuality.

5 or more "yes" answers: You are probably a cybersex addict, compulsively using digital sexual technology in ways that are out of control and negatively impacting your life. You will likely benefit from professional help.

Perhaps more important than the number of "yes" answers you had in the Cybersex Addiction Screening Test is how willing you are to be honest about all of this with yourself and at least one other person who is important to you. For instance, you may spend ten or twelve hours per week looking at online pornography, but if your spouse knows about this and is perfectly okay with it—if it doesn't violate or interfere with your personal and relationship commitments—then your porn use may not be a problem. In other words, if you are living honestly and have "sexual integrity" in your life, that integrity can be a mitigating factor in terms of a sex addiction diagnosis. If, however, you are spending ten or twelve hours per week using online porn, keeping this a secret from your spouse and other important people in your life, and you are no longer having sex with your spouse (who is concerned about this), then you're probably a sex addict.

As you can see, there are multiple factors that may or may not culminate in a sexual addiction diagnosis. As such, the Screening Test is more a guide than a definitive test. However, a "yes" answer to question 13, regarding illegal sexual activity, is always a problem, even if you're not a sex addict. If you answered "yes" to that question, you should absolutely seek confidential advice from a professional counselor who is skilled in handling these issues. Be aware when doing so that licensed professionals have reporting requirements that vary from state to state when it comes to illegal sexual behaviors, even those acted out only online.

Sex Addiction:
Is It a Legitimate Disorder?

The *Diagnostic and Statistical Manual of Mental Disorders,* also known as "the DSM," is published by the American Psychiatric Association (APA). In the United States, the DSM has historically been viewed as the "diagnostic bible" of psychiatric disorders. It was first published in 1952, and it is fully updated every dozen years or so, though minor revisions can occur at any time. Over the years, as psychiatrists' understanding of various behaviors has changed, there have been numerous additions and deletions to the DSM. For example, in 1968 homosexuality was listed as a mental disorder. A few years later, in 1973, the APA reversed its stance—and since that time the organization has worked hard to suppress the ignominy of ever having supported that idea. Currently sexual addiction is in a similar state of flux.

In the spring of 2013 the APA published the fifth major revision of the DSM (the DSM-5). Prior to publication, the organization considered Hypersexual Disorder (aka, sexual addiction) for inclusion as an official diagnosis. Noted psychiatrist and Harvard Medical School instructor Dr. Martin Kafka prepared the proposed diagnosis[1] for examination by the APA. In doing so, he reviewed the entire body of sex addiction-focused scientific research and literature, epidemiological and clinical, concluding:

> The data reviewed from these varying theoretical perspectives is compatible with the formulation that Hypersexual Disorder is a sexual desire disorder characterized by an increased frequency and intensity of sexually motivated fantasies, arousal, urges, and enacted behavior in association with an impulsivity component—a maladaptive behavioral response with adverse consequences. Hypersexual Disorder can be associated with vulnerability to dysphoric affects and the use of sexual behavior in response to dysphoric affects and/or life stressors associated with such affects. … Hypersexual Disorder is associated with increased time engaging in sexual fantasies and behaviors (sexual preoccupation/sexual obsession) and a significant degree of volitional impairment or "loss of control" characterized as disinhibition, impulsivity, compulsivity, or behavioral addiction. … [Hypersexual Disorder] can be accompanied by both clinically significant personal distress and social and medical morbidity.[2]

After reviewing decades of scientific research, analysis, and commentary, Dr. Kafka concluded that sexual addiction very definitely exists. Furthermore, he noted that sex addicts engage in their addictive fantasies and behaviors as a way to self-soothe emotional discomfort brought on by depression, anxiety, and unresolved early-life trauma. Lastly, he noted that sexual addiction typically results in significant distress and negative life consequences. So basically he confirmed what sex addiction treatment specialists have been saying for years—that there are three main elements to sexual addiction:

1. Sexual obsession
2. Loss of control
3. Negative consequences

Amazingly, the APA—inexplicably and without explanation—chose to disregard Dr. Kafka's presentation of the facts and to exclude Hypersexual Disorder from the DSM-5. Certainly we have theories as to why the APA has adopted this untenable stance. The kindest of these notions is that the organization feels there is not yet enough scientific evidence proving that sex can indeed become an addiction.

If the APA did in fact exclude sexual addiction from the DSM-5 based on a lack of scientific evidence, they won't be able to do so much longer, as new and powerful research has recently emerged in support of sexual addiction as a legitimate disorder. To date, two notable studies have been published post-Kafka, one looking at the efficacy of his proposed diagnostic criteria, the second examining the effects of sexual stimuli on the brain.

In the diagnostic criteria field trial,[3] researchers examined 207 patients at mental health clinics across the country. Psychological testing and interviews were conducted with each of the subjects, all of whom had sought treatment for hypersexual behavior, substance abuse, or another psychiatric condition such as depression or anxiety. The aim of the research was to learn if people who'd entered treatment for sexual addiction would be accurately identified by the Hypersexual Disorder criteria, and to make sure those who did not enter treatment seeking help with out-of-control sexual activity would not be misidentified as hypersexual. The study found that Dr. Kafka's criteria are indeed well constructed. The proposed diagnosis correctly identified 88% of the self-identified sexual addicts. More importantly, the diagnosis was 93% accurate in terms of negative results. Notably, many of the people seeking treatment for substance abuse issues reported also engaging in problematic sexual activity, but only when drunk or high, and the proposed diagnosis identified only one of these people as sexually addicted. For the rest, the primary disorder was recognized as substance abuse. This level of accuracy is actually quite high in comparison to most other psychiatric diagnoses.

The diagnostic field trial, while useful, is hardly definitive in proving the existence of sexual addiction. What we've really needed is scientific evidence that sexual addiction affects the brain in the same ways as other addictions. And in July of 2014 this proof arrived in the form of a detailed fMRI study conducted by researchers at Cambridge University (UK).[4] This study compared the brain activity of self-identified sex addicts to the brain activity of non-sex addicts, and also to the brain activity of drug addicts. The researchers found that when sex addicts are shown pornographic imagery their brains "light up" in three specific areas—the ventral striatum, the dorsal anterior cingulate, and the amygdala—while the brains of non-sex addicts do not. Furthermore, when sex addicts' brains light up they do so in the same places and to the same degree as the brains of drug addicts when they are exposed to drug-related stimuli. In short, the parts of the brain in charge of things like anticipatory pleasure, mood, memory, and decision-making are activated in sex addicts exactly as they are with drug addicts. Other variables in this study also linked sex addiction with other forms of addiction, though brain reactivity was by far the most important measure.

Despite the APA's current unwillingness to accept sexual addiction as a very real and devastating disorder, other organizations, most notably the American Society of Addiction Medicine (ASAM), have opted for a much more forward-thinking stance. ASAM writes:

> Addiction is a primary, chronic disease of brain reward, motivation, memory and related circuitry. Dysfunction in these circuits leads to characteristic biological, psychological, social and spiritual manifestations. This is reflected in an individual pathologically pursuing reward and/or relief by substance use *and other behaviors*. [Emphasis added.][5]

The studies discussed above, in particular the recent fMRI study, are significant proof that ASAM has it right when it comes to behavioral addictions—recognizing that they are in most respects no different than substance addictions.

So will the APA leap forward and legitimize sexual addiction with its first set of addendums to the DSM-5? Probably not. But they won't be able to hold out forever. In fact, Dr. Richard Krueger of Columbia University, who served on the physician committee that considered and ultimately rejected Hypersexual Disorder for inclusion in the DSM-5, has called the Cambridge fMRI research a "seminal study"[6] supporting the notion that sexual addiction is indeed an identifiable and diagnosable disorder. Eventually, it seems, the APA will be forced to accept the mounting proof that sexual addiction is a real, debilitating, diagnosable, and treatable disorder. Until that time, nothing much changes, meaning that clinicians who diagnose and treat sexual addiction will continue to do so in the ways they know best, with or without APA recognition.

WHY CAN'T I JUST SAY NO?

It is not unusual for people who have experienced chaos, neglect, inconsistency, abuse and/or trauma in childhood (even if they minimize that experience to themselves and others), to struggle with emotional maturity and adult relationship intimacy. Lacking the consistent experience of genuine nurturing that every child requires to emotionally mature, they learn early in life to cope with emotional or physical pain. They do this by using distraction and fantasy in childhood and later substance abuse and/or arousing, pleasurable distractions such as gambling, online gaming, shopping, or cybersex. These "self medicating" patterns, while useful as emotional avoidance/survival tools, further preclude the development of skills required to meet or even to recognize their healthy adult emotional needs. These individuals become proficient at using immediate gratification as a means of achieving temporary emotional stability and stress relief.

If you are addicted to a substance or a behavior, then you are likely someone who has difficultly recognizing, understanding, and managing your emotions and reactions. For you, irritability, anxiety, stress, embarrassment, and even joy are at times overwhelming. Or you may be someone who "doesn't feel" as much as normal people do, meaning you're not sad when it's time to be sad, or happy when it's time to be happy. The use of drugs, alcohol, and intensity-based behaviors (gambling, spending, video gaming, cybersex, etc.) is often the easiest way for you to tolerate these difficult emotional states. The classic example of the shy person who becomes the life of the party after a few drinks demonstrates clearly how an external input, in this case alcohol, can help a person manage emotional discomfort. Potentially addictive behaviors provide a similar coping mechanism.

Of course, not everyone who uses and enjoys sexnology is a cybersex addict. Just as there are casual or even heavy non-addicted drinkers, there are casual or even heavy non-addicted users of sexual technology. If you are a casual user, it is wise to be aware of your usage and to keep your eyes open for potential negative consequences. In the same way that a casual drinker should not drive home from the local pub after swigging a pint or two, a casual cybersex user should not engage in unprotected sex with strangers (no matter how "hot" they are). If you are an at-risk cybersex user, you should always be wary of what you are doing sexually, keeping in mind that you can sometimes behave like an addict—meaning you are perfectly capable of making some very bad sexual decisions with potentially life-altering consequences. Finally, if you believe you are sexually addicted, you should seek help right away, as addictions and their consequences only get worse without intervention and proper direction.

> *I was alone a lot when I was a kid. In fact, I think by age five or six I was pretty much what we used to call a latchkey kid. Every day after school I got home and I had the run of the house until at least 5:30, so I explored every nook and cranny. And it wasn't long before I found my dad's porn stash. I could have gone outside to play with other kids in the neighborhood, but I always felt different and apart from them, like there was no way they'd ever want to hang out with me. But I had my dad's porn. I know now that I wasn't ready for anything that explicit, but it was there and I looked at it. A lot. And there was plenty to look at, too. Dad kept entire stacks of sex magazines, never just one or two. A few years later, when I started my own porn collection as a teenager, downloading the images and videos I found online, I just figured, "like father, like son." Today I have tens of thousands of por- nographic images on my hard drive. I'm ashamed of this, and I know it keeps me from dating and having a regular sex life, but I can't seem to stop myself. Plus, porn is always there for me. No matter how bad*

*I'm feeling, it never lets me down and it always ends in some kind of
pleasure and comfort. All in all, I think I'm pretty hooked on the stuff.*
                                          —Jeff, thirty-four, salesperson

People who carry deep emotional wounds tend to more often *react to
their emotions* rather than thinking through their decisions. By definition,
this means they tend to be more impulsive, seeking to *feel better now*
while dismissing and denying potential long-term consequences of their
actions. While healthy people under stress are likely to take a deep breath,
go for a walk or run, take a long bath, talk to a friend, read distracting
literature, or even watch TV to feel better, emotionally wounded people,
when presented with emotionally triggering or stressful situations, tend to
move toward stimulation and distraction. If the distraction they use is both
effective in relieving their uncomfortable feelings, albeit temporarily, and
simultaneously *pleasurable* to them, they understandably return to it over
and over.

With potentially pleasurable addictive substances and activities, a
healthy person might say, "I did this once and it didn't turn out so well,
so there's no need to do it again," or, "No thanks, I can see where this is
heading and I don't want to go there." In fact, most people who've used a
substance or behavior in a way that resulted in or even risked a negative
outcome will recognize the potential for future disaster and adjust their
behaviors accordingly. But emotionally wounded people often ignore the
potential consequences of their actions in favor of a newfound temporary
pleasurable escape. For them, repetitively engaging in dopamine-releasing
activities such as substance abuse, bingeing on junk food, or engaging in
cybersex becomes their "go-to" means of controlling emotional discomfort.
Over time, as they repeatedly lose themselves in the intensely arousing
feelings produced by these pleasurable distractions, addiction rears its
ugly head.

OUTWARD MANIFESTATIONS OF ADDICTION

All addictions—whether to substances (alcohol, tobacco, prescription medications, illicit drugs) or behaviors (gambling, shopping, gaming, sex, romance)—are characterized by three behavioral elements, all of which must be present to define and diagnose addiction.

1. **Preoccupation or obsession:** The person spends large, often increasing amounts of time and/or money thinking about, planning, or actually doing the behavior.

2. **Loss of control over the activity:** The behavior has become compulsive and the person has lost the ability to stop when he or she wishes, although the person may not willingly admit this to self or others. The individual may have unsuccessfully tried to curtail or stop the behavior on one or more occasions.

3. **Continuation despite negative consequences:** Negative consequences may include relationship problems, job loss, educational issues, physical or emotional health concerns, loss of interest in previously enjoyable activities, legal trouble, and more.

When these three criteria are met, a person is most likely suffering from an addictive disorder to either a substance or a pleasure-inducing behavior. Another typical characteristic of addiction (although not always present) is *tolerance*, meaning it takes more and more of the substance or activity to achieve the same effect. For instance, drug addicts often find themselves using increasing amounts of their drug of choice, or switching to a "harder" drug in an effort to experience the same high they're used to. Similarly, pathological gamblers bet larger amounts of money, play for longer periods, or hit the casino more often. And those addicted to tech-driven sexual fantasies and behavior typically find themselves spending more time engaged in those activities and/or seeking out increasingly more intense, arousing, and sometimes disturbing experiences.

Addicts of all types can become irritable, even outright angry, if asked to stop their addictive behaviors. In other words, addicts tend to be highly defensive of their addiction, especially if they have been secretive about it. They tend to blame the people trying to help them for making them angry, often calling friends and loved ones intrusive, prudish, nagging, or worse. Due to their obsessive relationship with whatever it is that they're addicted to, they are rarely able to see or consider in the moment how their behavior is affecting others, even those close to them. For all addicts, the relationship to their "drug or behavior of choice" gradually becomes far more important than anyone else's feelings or opinions—at least until a crisis hits.

CHAPTER THREE

THE CONSEQUENCES OF SEX GONE AWRY

I am facing a potential separation and divorce from a woman I deeply love because of multiple extramarital affairs initiated via smartphone hookup apps. It started out really innocently, with me just "playing" and enjoying the fact that women other than my wife found me attractive. But before I knew it, I had three different women that I was seeing regularly! It was never my intention to lose my marriage, but I haven't been able to stop the behavior that's destroying it.

—Pete, thirty-seven, mechanic

I am addicted to Internet porn and compulsive masturbation. I can't seem to walk away from it even though I really want to. I am tired of living in a fantasy world and I want a real relationship with a person who cares about me. But the only "relationships" I've ever had have been these online fantasies and the occasional app-based hookup. Honestly, I have no idea how to initiate or follow through on a romantic relationship with real people in the real world. I honestly feel completely lost about things everybody else seems to understand intuitively.

—Diane, thirty-four, physician

Most short-term, immediately gratifying, pleasurable activities have the potential to become addictive in some people. Moreover, the accessibility, affordability, anonymity, and interactivity of certain tech-driven behaviors only increases that potential. Among these potential "red-alert" problem areas is sexual activity. Digital technology makes cybersex hyper-available and hyper-exciting, and therefore hyper-addictive. With every new advance in digital technology this becomes a greater reality. Unfortunately, all of this escapist sexual pleasure, when it becomes addictive, leads to serious consequences for those who are hooked and also for the people around them.

Typical consequences of tech-driven sexual addiction include the following:

- Isolation (from dating, family, and social interaction in general)
- Reduced intimacy, sexuality, and communication with one's committed partner (caused by lies, manipulation, and physical/emotional unavailability)
- Broken trust in existing relationships, sometimes leading to separation or divorce
- Increased stress levels related to living a secretive and compartmentalized life
- Feeling shameful, guilty, and stressed about lies and justifications for sexual activity
- Feeling shameful, guilty, and stressed about failed promises to stop or change one's sexual behavior
- Mistrust, hurt, and anger in those close to the addict
- Potential job loss or problems in school related to either acting out or to decreased productivity
- Contracting or spreading sexually transmitted diseases (STDs)
- Risking physical danger/violence by hooking up with anonymous, unknown strangers
- Unwanted pregnancy (and possibly abortion)
- Partners losing self-esteem and self-worth by trying and failing to "measure up" to fantasy porn images or extramarital lovers
- Children inadvertently being exposed to sexual activity or pornography when they step into a room while a parent is involved

in cybersex activities, or when they find sexual content on a parent's computer, laptop, smartphone, or another digital device

- Ignoring or emotionally neglecting spouses, children, other family members, and friends
- Sexual dysfunction in men, such as erectile dysfunction, delayed ejaculation, or an inability to reach orgasm
- Loss of interest in previously enjoyable hobbies and other healthy activities, such as exercise or spending time with friends and family
- Self-neglect due to lack of sleep, lack of exercise, and eating poorly
- Financial issues
- Legal issues, including arrest

EMOTIONAL PROBLEMS

All that time online landed me with a lot of guilt and shame, both of which led to isolation and loneliness. Cybersex addiction was a part of my life that I could not and did not want to share with my wife. It drove a wedge between us. I was depressed because I felt trapped and unable to break free from my obsession, and I also felt that I was pushing away from the person I would normally turn to for just about anything. It was scary.

—James, forty-five, businessman

Cybersex addicts live with the constant emotional challenge of keeping themselves afloat while leading a double-life. Keeping secrets, minimizing, altering situations and circumstances to cover up the truth—including blatantly lying about simple things such as where they've been, what they've been doing, and even how they feel—are all constants for active cybersex and porn addicts. Many admit that it feels as if they are living two lives—a hidden one taking place in a shadow world of images, videos, avatars, webcams, and app-driven hookups, and another that takes place in the real world of work, family, and friends. In short, having a singular focus on sex creates a dissociative gap that widens over time.

As their acting out continues, sex addicts can become increasingly irritable, controlling, withdrawn, and exhausted. By the time they seek help, they typically show signs of profound anxiety, depression, and emotional exhaustion—driven by the stress of maintaining their ongoing lies coupled with shame, despair, and self-hatred about what they are doing. Plus, there is the constant and nagging fear of being found out. So even though sex addicts initially act out as a way to escape emotional discomfort and the pain of underlying psychological issues, what they actually do is create more serious problems and even deeper emotional turmoil.

RELATIONSHIP PROBLEMS

My sex addiction created a wall between my husband and me. I avoided conversation so I wouldn't have to answer any questions about what I was doing, and I told all sorts of lies about working late, traveling for work, and where all the money was going. As for our intimate relationship, all the flirtation and sex with other men resulted in less sexual attention toward my husband. He became less interesting and less attractive to me with every affair or one-night stand I carried out. Eventually we didn't talk or interact at all, except to fight.

—Melissa, fifty, university professor

Cybersex addiction can produce tremendously destructive consequences for those in a committed relationship. Obsession with external sexual activity leaves emotional and physical intimacy flat and drained of meaning for both partners. Sexuality, affection, honesty, and bonding all suffer as the addict becomes increasingly fixated on carrying out and hiding addictive sexual experiences. Spouses and significant others, often in the dark about the problem and confused by the emotional and physical distance that has suddenly appeared in their relationship, sometimes blame themselves for the problems, judging themselves to be sexually or physically or otherwise inadequate.

Complicating matters is the fact that digital relationships—chat-room encounters, webcam sex, flirting on social media, and sexting—are often rationalized as "not really cheating" because they don't take place in person and there is no "actual sex." Digital affairs can be easily denied to a spouse with statements like these:

- I've never even met her, so how can you say I'm cheating?
- I'm never going to meet him. I don't even know his last name.
- We've never touched each other or had anything close to "real" sex.
- It's just a playful distraction, a game, so what's the big deal?
- I don't even know where they live.

Nevertheless, digital betrayals are acutely painful to a cheated-on spouse—every bit as much as an in-the-flesh affair. Still, people who sexually act out via digital technology nearly always rely on the "it's not really cheating" excuse as part of their denial. Only later, when forced to deal with their partner's feelings of deep betrayal, diminished self-esteem, anger, depression, distancing, and thoughts of ending the relationship do they come to understand that secretive extramarital sexual activity that only takes place online is still cheating. Lying and keeping sexual secrets from an intimate, committed partner qualifies as infidelity no matter where it takes place.

DISRUPTION OF FAMILY LIFE

Because of my cybersex addiction, I was spending less and less time playing with my children after work and on weekends, and I had been such an active dad before all this started. But once I got into the online sex and hookup apps, instead of joining the family after work, I would use apps to hook up or I'd hole up in the den on my laptop until late in the evening, sometimes even skipping dinner. I gradually got less involved in figuring out the usual household dilemmas, the childcare balancing act, and helping with the kids' homework. My wife tells me now that sometimes she was concerned about leaving the kids with me when she went out to run errands, as I would get so involved with what I was doing online that I never really watched them. She was afraid that I wouldn't hear them if they needed me.

—Will, thirty-five, attorney

In relationships where compulsive sexual activity has become a priority for one of the partners, family life suffers. Basic responsibilities of childcare and family involvement lose precedence, becoming secondary to the emotional distractions of digital sexuality. When a spouse is online for hours on end, bills go unpaid, property and income taxes are ignored, and the basic management of the home shifts from a shared activity to the shoulders of the non-addicted partner. So in addition to creating problems within a primary relationship, tech-driven sexual addiction negatively affects all other aspects of family life.

One of the biggest family-life concerns typically centers on young children being directly exposed to pornography or sexual activity.

> *I know the boys have found porn on my laptop and maybe even some of the pictures that women have sexted to me that I've got stored on my phone. A couple of months ago I found some porn pages bookmarked on my eleven-year-old's computer—the same pages I had bookmarked on my own—but I felt too ashamed to speak to him or my wife about it. I just ignored it. And both our boys have walked in on me while I was online looking at porn. My youngest even told me to "take those pictures off the computer," that "it's gross." I think both boys have lost respect for me.*
>
> —Armand, forty-two, accountant

Of course, regardless of whether children of cybersex addicts are directly exposed to pornography or sexual activity, they may wonder where all of their caregiver's time is going and why that caregiver no longer seems to care about them as much as they once did. Some wonder what they did wrong to lose the attention of mom or dad. In other words, children of sex addicts are harmed by the addict's emotional unavailability and sometimes even outright neglect. Furthermore, sex addiction often creates parental tension and arguments, which can also significantly and negatively impact children.

POOR SELF-CARE

Every night I waited until my roommate was asleep, and then I'd go on dating sites and started chatting with all sorts of men. Sometimes I would even sneak out of our apartment to meet them for sex. Always I would tell myself, I'm just going online for a few minutes to see who's still awake and maybe say hello. But then, before I knew it, three or four hours would disappear. Sometimes I would only stop when I saw the sun coming up. I got more and more exhausted as my addiction progressed, and I was physically ill a lot because of that. I stopped going to the gym and eating right because that stuff took time and energy that I no longer possessed. Nevertheless, I totally ignored the fact that staying up all night to act out was an issue.

—Amy, twenty-eight, schoolteacher

As addictions progress, there is less and less time to focus on proper self-care and physical maintenance. To avoid confrontations from a concerned spouse or friend, cybersex addicts will often give up precious hours of rest to seek out sexual activity. They may stay awake long after others have gone to bed or get up in the middle of the night to go online or check their phone apps for hits. "I'll just stay up for a few more minutes" turns into hours spent searching for the next perfect image or person. Even those who don't stay up late to sexually act out can find their formerly healthy sleep patterns increasingly disrupted by the anxiety and fear created by their addiction. This lack of sleep can lead to illness, increased stress, decreased productivity, and, sadly, a desire to self-medicate with further acting out.

Sadly, sex addicts will often replace healthy self-care with sexual acting out. Doctor visits, dentist appointments, exercise, preparing and eating healthy meals, and more take a backseat to sexual addiction. Furthermore, Internet chat rooms and smartphone hookup apps create an atmosphere of immediacy and intensity in which concerns about safety and self-care are often forgotten. Occasionally, resolution of this intense arousal state can be satisfied only by IRL encounters with casual, anonymous, or paid-for partners—some of whom may be dangerous people or infected with sexually transmitted diseases. And while it is true that you can't get an STD from viewing porn or having webcam sex, over time a significant percentage of porn and cybersex addicts escalate from digital to IRL encounters. In one survey, 40 percent of the people who self-identified as being "addicted to cybersex" reported eventually progressing to IRL sexual encounters.[1]

SEXUAL DYSFUNCTION

My long-term girlfriend and I are both graduate students, but at separate universities located about an hour and a half apart. Typically we spend weekends together, using the weekdays to focus on our schoolwork. Our sex life was great until about a year ago, and I'm not sure what happened. I used to look forward to her visits because I knew the first thing we would do was hop in bed and make love. But lately I struggle to reach orgasm when I'm with her. I've even faked it a couple of times just to get things over with. What I can't understand is why I'm ready, willing, and able when I log onto my favorite porn sites, but I can't function when I've got the real thing right there in front of me. My girlfriend is incredibly sexy, and I'm not at all bored with her. I just can't perform with her the way I'm supposed to.

—Mark, twenty-six, graduate student

For some people, abuse of online pornography interferes with their ability to develop and maintain healthy romantic and sexual partnerships. In fact, porn addiction seems to lead not only to an emotional disconnect but also to a physical disconnect. In the example above, Mark is suffering from delayed ejaculation (DE), a problem that is more common than most people realize. Symptoms of DE include taking longer than normal to reach orgasm, being able to reach orgasm only via masturbation, and not being able to reach orgasm at all. Many younger men who suffer from DE don't mind at first because "lasting longer" is generally viewed as a sign of maturity and/or virility. Unfortunately, as Mark and many others have discovered, there really is such a thing as "too much of a good thing."

As with all sexual dysfunctions, there are numerous possible causes of DE, including physical illness or impairment, use of some antidepressants that are known to delay and sometimes even eliminate orgasm, and psychological stressors such as financial worries and job issues. One other increasingly documented cause is abuse of pornography and compulsive masturbation. Porn induced erectile dysfunction is becoming more and more common, especially in young men. And clinicians are taking notice of this. The good news is that there is help for people like Mark who are otherwise healthy and in the prime of their life. By stopping the artificial stimuli (the porn) and instead focusing on building and nurturing real person relationships, it is possible to retrain and reboot your brain. Go to www.yourbrainonporn.com to learn more. [2]

So it appears that the digitally driven tsunami of accessible, affordable, and increasingly graphic pornography can lead to various forms of sexual dysfunction, especially in men. In all likelihood this problem is not simply due to the frequency of masturbation and orgasm outside a primary relationship; it is perhaps more related to the fact that men in general are turned on by new stimuli. The man who spends 75 percent of his sexual life masturbating to porn is, over time, likely to find his longer-term partner less sexually stimulating than the constant variety of new and exciting material in his head. So what we are now seeing is an emotional disconnect with spouses and partners that is manifesting physically as sexual dysfunction, be it DE or its better known cousin, erectile dysfunction (ED).

As mentioned in chapter one, at least a few porn and cybersex addicts eventually find themselves "out of sync" with real world relationships. Some of those people may actually be losing interest in real world intimacy altogether. Consider, for instance, the results of two 1,500-person studies in Japan, one conducted in 2008, the other in 2010.[3] These studies found that in 2010, 36.1 percent of males ages sixteen to nineteen had no interest in or an outright aversion to sex with another person. This figure was more than double the result of the 2008 survey (17.5 percent). For males ages twenty to twenty-four, the percentage increase was similar, rising from 11.8 percent to 21.5 percent. Not surprisingly, this decreased interest in real world sexual encounters coincides directly with the "tech-connect" boom that has given rise to social media, consumer-generated porn, built-in webcams, smartphone hookup apps, and the like.

In another study, this one looking at the effects of tech-driven sex addiction on the lives of married or otherwise committed couples, one-third of the cybersex addicts said they were no longer interested in sex with their partner.[4] The partners (mostly female) reported hearing consistent excuses like, "I'm not in the mood," "I'm too tired," "I've been working too hard," "The children might hear," or "My back hurts." Sometimes the sex addict would admit to having already had an orgasm that day and not wanting sex again. Even when there was a sexual spark, the cybersex-abusing spouse was described as distant, emotionally detached, and interested only in his or her own pleasure. The non-cybersex-abusing partners said they typically ended up doing most or all of the sexual initiating, either to get their own needs met or in a hopeful attempt to get the addict to decrease his or her online sexual activity. These partners—already feeling hurt, angry, sexually rejected, left out, and inadequate—reported that they also frequently felt responsible for the couple's sexual problems. In some cases they just went along with whatever sex was offered, whenever it was offered, even when they weren't in the mood or found a particular sexual act objectionable, all to avoid being thought of as "boring" or "not sexy."

TROUBLE AT WORK

My company gives everyone a work-issued laptop and smartphone, along with very specific instructions on how those devices are and are not to be used. "No pornography" and "No sexual websites/apps" are right there at the top of the rules list. But I figured that if I wasn't looking at porn during work hours, and I wasn't sneaking away for sex during work hours, they really wouldn't care what I was up to. Most likely they would understand that I was a single gay guy, and I was going to be sexual. Still, I was definitely wasting time at work because even though I wasn't meeting people for sex, I had hookup apps turned on 24/7 and I would respond to guys and make dates for that night throughout the workday. After the human resources director wrote me up the first time for misusing my laptop, I kept things completely on my phone. But it turns out the tech people at work could easily track everything I was doing on that, too. I got fired the second time they caught me, even though I really needed the job.

—Raif, twenty-eight, sales manager

Using work-issued digital devices for sexual purposes is dangerous business—a lesson Raif and many others often learn the hard way. Most companies have written rules regarding such behavior. Typically, human resource policies include a verbal or written warning for the first offense, followed by immediate dismissal for a recurrence. Unfortunately, sex and love addicts hooked on the thrill of looking at and/or seeking sexual material will often justify their use of office equipment for such purposes by telling themselves, "They won't find out it was me," or, "I only do this on breaks and after hours, never on company time," or, "Everybody does this."

In the early years of the Internet, some tolerant businesses looked the other way at such behavior. Now, however, companies are actively prohibiting the use of company-owned digital devices for sexual and romantic purposes—not just in the work environment but everywhere else, too. There is actually a federal law that specifically permits an employer to monitor and review an employee's digital interactions on company equipment both in and out of the workplace.

Some company-issued devices come with Internet filtering and accountability software designed to limit and/or monitor the digital wanderings of workers. On top of this, personal computers, laptops, smartphones, and other digital devices are now routinely scanned for misuse when undergoing regular maintenance or upgrades. Employees who are unable or unwilling to change their unacceptable behaviors face humiliation, embarrassment, a poor work record, and even dismissal.

Nevertheless, many companies fail to adequately address cybersex problems properly when they become evident in the workplace. Yes, over the past several decades human resources and employee assistance programs have become more knowledgeable about addiction-related employee behavior issues. Some have implemented standard and highly informed responses to problems such as alcoholism and drug abuse, ranging from worker education to actual interventions. Today, HR and EAP specialists understand that warnings and slaps on the wrist are unlikely to cause behavior change in addicts, that instead these individuals need direct and immediate help including referrals to treatment facilities and Twelve Step support groups. Unfortunately, the same compassionate corporate intervention is rarely available to workers who bring sexual addiction into the workplace.

Consider the case of John, a thirty-three-year-old physical therapist who worked at a rehabilitation clinic. After John was discovered viewing pornography on his work computer, he was given a written warning, which included a statement that if the problem recurred he'd be fired. However, there were no recommendations for further evaluation or treatment. Had John been found drinking on the job, the outcome would have been quite different. Most likely he would have been offered the choice to either seek help (treatment) or leave his job. As it was, John stayed away from sexual sites on his work computer but otherwise continued his life and sexual behaviors as if nothing problematic had happened. Four months later, one of John's physical therapy patients accurately accused him of making subtle but nonetheless clear sexual advances toward her while he was providing physical therapy. He was immediately fired, his physical therapy license was revoked, and his company ended up settling a lawsuit with the patient for a large sum of money.

Had John been immediately referred to counseling when his cybersex problem first appeared at work through his use of online porn, there would have been a professional assessment and support that allowed for a more situation-appropriate response. This might have prevented the problems that later occurred, including the negative consequences of losing his job and his license to practice physical therapy—and perhaps the victim would have been spared this personal violation.

FINANCIAL ISSUES

I spent money traveling, buying gifts for the women I was meeting, paying for dinners, staying in motels, and even maintaining a second iPhone in an effort to hide my behaviors from my girlfriend of eleven years—outlays that drained our bank account to the point where I finally had to tell her where the money was actually going. Now I'm terrified she's going to leave me. I'm not sure if she's madder that I was cheating or that I was spending so much money doing it. Plus, on more than one occasion I've used my company expense account to treat women to expensive dinners and gifts. So I live in constant fear that someone will take a good look at my work expenses and that will be the end of a job I truly love.

—Lydia, forty-four, pharmaceutical sales rep

In the pre-digital (analog) world, a sex addict who compulsively collected porn could end up purchasing hundreds of magazines and movies, spending thousands of dollars in the process. Other forms of casual sexual activity were also extremely expensive. For instance, in the 1980s through the early 2000s people paid for "phone sex" at $1.99 per minute, sometimes owing thousands of dollars per month. And at strip clubs, mandatory drinks and tips for dancers—not to mention the price of a lap dance or two—could add up to hundreds of dollars per visit. Even those more focused on romantic intensity needed to cough up money, paying for personal ads along with expensive dates and dating services.

With the digital technology explosion, casual sex and romantic intrigue are much more affordable. Porn is now almost infinitely available at no cost, webcams present strip shows free, and dating and hookup apps are either free or very inexpensive. Today, sex and love addicts can act out almost indefinitely at little to no cost, removing a significant barrier to the nearly constant search for intensity and emotional escape.

That said, tech-driven sex and romance can still get expensive if you're not careful about what you're doing. In-person meetings can be quite costly. And in a single online sitting, porn users can spend hundreds of dollars on live video feeds, live sexual chat with paid models, streaming videos, and virtual sex games. Some sexual sites charge by the minute on top of a monthly or annual membership fee. And it is not unusual for cybersex addicts, in a moment of shameful determination, to cancel their memberships and delete all of their downloaded porn and sexual contacts. Of course, within a few days those same people suddenly "find themselves" coughing up still more money to sign back on, thereby starting the whole process all over again. Over time, cybersex addicts can easily spend thousands of dollars a month on their addictive behaviors.

LEGAL ISSUES

After graduating from college, I was offered a great job in a city several hours away from the small town where I grew up. I did well at my job and got a quick promotion. I even bought my own condo, which hardly anyone my age does. But I had no friends nearby, and as a result I was constantly lonely. In my early teens, I'd discovered porn, and in retrospect I used it compulsively when I could. But back then, with family around and school to deal with, I didn't have enough opportunity for it to become a problem. I would go online, look at pictures for a few minutes, masturbate, and then move on to something else. But now, as an adult living on my own without friends or a girlfriend, I had time to fully engage with pornography. At first it was all pretty vanilla, the same sort of stuff I'd been looking at as a kid. I would leave work, pick up some food, come home, and turn on my laptop. Before long I was spending four or five hours a night masturbating to porn, and what I was looking at got increasingly more intense, including some pretty extreme bondage stuff, and also images of underage girls.

Eventually I started hoarding porn secretly in a work computer file, masturbating during lunch breaks and after hours while still at the office. Unexpectedly one evening, a coworker spotted me and reported what she'd seen. I was fired right away, and when the technology guys went through my work computer, they found a couple of the illegal (underage) images I'd downloaded, along with a bunch of other pics, which they forwarded to the police. Now I'm unemployed and I might end up in jail as a sex offender. And the worst part is that I don't even really understand how it all happened. One day I was doing great, looking at a little bit of harmless porn to blow off steam, and the next day I was hooked on stuff I'm embarrassed to even talk about and would never even think about doing in real life.

—Zach, twenty-six, architect

Because of sex addiction's natural tendency to escalate, some men and women may "find themselves" engaged in illegal online sexual activities—everything from hiring prostitutes to viewing child pornography. Oftentimes, when these people are caught, they are shocked to finally realize where their addiction has led them.

HOW DO I STOP?

Unfortunately, nearly all cybersex addicts put off seeking help for their problematic behaviors until the consequences of their addiction have become so severe that they are forced to "wake up" to the full nature of the obvious problems they have created. Typically, they are only roused from their sexual stupor by an extreme external consequence. Rarely do they respond to any internal thought or feeling. In other words, emotional problems, neglect of health and self-care, and family dysfunction rarely motivate change. Instead, most cybersex addicts recognize their problem and seek help only after they've experienced relationship blowups, job loss, legal problems, or severe financial difficulties.

CHAPTER FOUR

SEXUAL ADDICTION: AN EQUAL OPPORTUNITY DISORDER FOR WOMEN TOO

I've been hooking up with men using the Ashley Madison app for more than two years. Recently, my husband found out what I've been up to, though he really has no idea how many men I've actually been with. I love him and I don't want to lose him, but at the same time I just get such a rush from being wanted by another man. It's sad, but my marriage feels really stale in comparison to the excitement of constantly dating and falling for someone new.

—Marie, twenty-six, computer programmer

Cybersex and searching online for intense romance, which started out as a kind of game, ended up consuming me. I got to the point where just closing my eyes for a few minutes would bring up all sorts of fantasies, and before I knew it I'd be back online, back into "the trance." After a while the faces and profiles of the men I met and chatted with on dating sites, hookup apps, and social media sites would haunt me. I got to where I couldn't look at a man anywhere without thinking about him undressed or without some other filthy thought coming into my mind.

—Jeannie, forty-one, clothing designer

In his groundbreaking book, *Don't Call It Love*, Dr. Patrick Carnes noted that about 3 to 5 percent of the adult population struggled with some form of addictive sexual behavior.[1] At that time, sex addicts were mostly men and as such we have few studies on female sex addicts. More recent research, plus a great deal of anecdotal evidence, indicates that the problem of sexual addiction online is now both escalating and becoming more evenly distributed among men and women.

WOMEN AND CYBERSEX ADDICTION

Although many assume that addictive sex is primarily a problem for men, about twenty-five percent of the members of Twelve Step recovery programs for sex and love addiction are women. Sadly, there is not yet a formalized process for identifying, diagnosing, and treating women who struggle with sexual addiction. This deficiency is related, in part, to the failure of many mental health and addiction professionals to recognize the subtleties of addictive and impulsive sexual behavior patterns in women. Often sex addiction in women is identified only after they've entered treatment for an eating disorder, substance abuse, or some other issue and then behaved in compulsively sexual ways while in treatment.

Most of the time, men's sexual acting out is overtly sexual and easily recognizable. Conversely, female sex addicts tend to view their behaviors in terms of "romance" and "relationships." Consequently, women who struggle with problematic patterns of sexual activity are more likely to enter therapy reporting intimacy or relationship-oriented problems than a problem with actual sex. Symptoms typically reported by female sex addicts include the following:

- A history of short, failed relationships where sex is the primary bond
- A pattern of returning to or remaining with partners who are abusive or emotionally unavailable
- Having a lot of casual sex but thinking of it as the road to a primary, intimate relationship

- Masturbating compulsively to romantic fantasies of past or potential partners, romantic books, fictional characters, television shows, and movies
- A pattern of inappropriate sexual relationships—with married men, bosses, or subordinates
- Consistently having sex as a way to feel wanted, loved, and validated
- Taking money or encouraging gift-giving in exchange for sex but not viewing this as prostitution
- Turning to prostitution as a cover for addictive sexual problems, perhaps reenacting a sexual abuse history
- Paying to visit unethical massage therapists and physical trainers in exchange for sex, but not viewing this as hiring prostitutes
- Excessively and consistently abusing food, exercise, and spending to "feel better" when lonely or not in a relationship
- Secretly acting out fetish behaviors with casual or anonymous partners while in a primary relationship
- A pattern of seeking emotional validation through online or in-person encounters (new relationships) while already in a primary relationship
- A pattern of using weight gain to push away intimate partners, but then losing the weight and becoming hypersexual when slim

Complicating matters in terms of identifying, diagnosing, and treating female sex addicts is our cultural gender bias toward sexual behavior. Men who have a lot of sex are called "players" and "studs." Rarely are compulsively sexual men portrayed in the media as people who are suffering from deeply rooted, painful psychological issues—the movies *Shame* and *Thanks for Sharing* being notable and well-executed exceptions. A similarly realistic look at female sexual addiction is provided in the 2014 movie *Nymphomaniac, Volume 1*. Women—even those who are not sexually addicted but nonetheless enjoy an active sex life—are often culturally denigrated and shamed as "sluts" and "whores."

Unfortunately, thanks to "cultural norms," women just aren't as willing as men to talk about their issues with hypersexual behavior. A man who has anonymous sex several times per week and uses masturbation for self-soothing and emotional escape may readily come to identify as a sex addict, especially if his sexual behavior begins to have serious consequences. Furthermore, a well-trained clinician is likely to identify him as such in therapy or treatment. Conversely, a woman who "finds herself" consistently seeking "love and affection" with strangers via chat rooms, on Facebook, or on dating sites like Match.com and eHarmony may have anonymous sex and masturbate just as frequently as her male counterpart, but she will probably not self-identify as having a "sexual problem." Nor is she likely to be diagnosed as such. Nevertheless, the disorder does exist in women, and it is every bit as problematic for them as it is for men—maybe even more so because female sex addicts are generally more vulnerable to rape and other forms of sexual violence.

Interestingly, among sexually compulsive users of the Internet, women are much more likely than men to progress from online encounters to real world partners. One study of both male and female cybersex addicts found that 80 percent of the women surveyed expressed a willingness to move from an online experience to a live one, while only 30 percent of the men expressed that desire.[2] This finding supports the notion that women are more attracted to mutual sexual activities—the give-and-take of a live encounter—than are men, who typically use digital technology to engage in non-intimate objectified sexual experiences.

> *I spend about twenty hours a week on Facebook, in chat rooms, and using smartphone apps to meet men. This is time that I used to spend with my husband and kids. I meet men online and chat with them, sending IMs, texting, sexting, and fantasizing that they're the perfect guy for me. Eventually we arrange to meet in person, usually at a motel or some other place where we can have sex. By then of course I'm already attached emotionally, and that scares the men off. They just want sex. I can't seem to develop a meaningful relationship with any*

of them. Basically we just have sex a few times and then it's over. None of the relationships have lasted more than a month.

Meanwhile, I'm completely unavailable emotionally to my husband, and I've even withdrawn from my kids. It feels like I've abandoned my entire family, but I can't stop what I'm doing. I keep imagining that someday one of these men will really love me, and I shut out the hurt I experience every time it doesn't work out. I keep searching for that passion. I want to be loved by the perfect man, even though I know intellectually that person doesn't exist. I love the sex, of course, but what I really crave is the attention.

—Janice, thirty-five, public relations manager

Like many lonely women, Janice is driven by a fantasy of connection. This is quite evident in the way that she views her IRL encounters—as "relationships," even though none have lasted longer than a few "dates." In actuality, her brief affairs are not so much relationships as extended one-night stands that end whenever the man she's hooked up with decides to move on.

WOMEN AND PORN

Historically, men have used pornography far more often than women. One 2006 study of 10,000 randomly sampled people ages eighteen to forty-nine found that 82 percent of those surveyed had looked at pornographic magazines, 84 percent had viewed pornographic films, and 34 percent had viewed porn on the Internet.[3] Keep in mind, this study was conducted in 2006—a lifetime ago in Internet years. Back then, the most significant variable for predicting who had used porn was gender. And the gender difference was most pronounced on the Internet, with 63 percent of the men but only 13.6 percent of women stating they had viewed porn online. Again, this was way back in 2006. The numbers would likely be much, much higher today.

Perhaps this study's "gender gap" was caused by the nature of the available pornography. After all, it is well-known that men are more visually stimulated while women are more aroused by emotional connections and relationships (both fantasized and actual). In other words, men are more likely to be turned on by an endless stream of sexualized and objectified body parts while women are more likely to become aroused by the presence (or at least the perceived presence) of emotional intimacy. And at the time of the 2006 study, female-oriented porn—aka, relationship-oriented "mommy porn," such as the best-selling novel *Fifty Shades of Grey*, its two bestselling sequels, and the ongoing plethora of knockoffs—had not yet hit the scene.

The Fifty Shades trilogy traces the relationship between beautiful Anastasia Steele and super-sexy but emotionally troubled billionaire Christian Grey. If this sounds like a Harlequin romance novel, that's not surprising. In many ways the Fifty Shades books fit nicely into the lengthy romance novel tradition of naïve young virgins being seduced by otherworldly bad boys. However, in most romance novels the sex scenes fade to black well before the proverbial money shot, while the Fifty Shades books track the action, in graphic detail, all the way to and through its oh-so-sweetly orgasmic conclusion.

Both reader reviews and anecdotal evidence suggest the vast majority of the Fifty Shades trilogy's mostly female following is entranced not so much by the graphic depictions of sex as by the development of the emotional relationship between the two main characters. A similar phenomenon, aimed at a younger female demographic, is the equally successful Twilight book and film series, with its exploration of sexy but emotionally flawed male figures presented as vampires and werewolves struggling with their desire to possess a young girl. Dr. Patrick Carnes discusses the parallels of these two books in his popular Fifty Shades of Twilight lecture.

Of course, mommy porn doesn't do it for all women. In fact, a growing number of women are viewing and masturbating to highly objectified hardcore pornography, just like men. These women are perfectly comfortable viewing men or women in terms of their body parts, and they are very clear in the idea that when they are online they are looking for a solo sexual encounter and *not* any type of relationship. Today, a third of all

Internet porn users are women,[4] up from 14 percent in 2003.[5] So it seems that females are taking advantage of the Internet's easy, affordable, and anonymous access to pornography, which allows them to view culturally shamed imagery and stories in the privacy of their home.

This increased access to explicit, objectified sexual material is for many women a breath of fresh air, allowing them to explore their sexual fantasies and urges in ways that until recently didn't exist. Unfortunately, as is the case for men, there are women who learn over time to use sexual/romantic objectification as a way to escape reality and dissociate from life's stressors. For these women, pornography can become a "drug of choice," used to self-regulate and feel a sense of control over uncomfortable emotional states. This behavior can easily escalate to the level of sexual addiction, eventually resulting, as all addictions do, in serious negative life consequences. In this crucial way, women's increased access to and interest in highly objectified hardcore pornography presents the same concerns as it does for men.

PORN IS THE TIP OF THE ICEBERG

Like male cybersex addicts, sexually addicted women use digital technology to access much more than just pornography. They go on social media to flirt and be sexual, they sext with reckless abandon, they use "friend finder" apps to locate casual and anonymous sex partners, they cruise websites looking for prostitutes and erotic masseuses, they exhibit themselves using webcams, they mutually masturbate online, they play "adult" video games, and more. In short, sexual addiction is an equal opportunity disease, afflicting anyone and everyone with equal ferocity, resulting in negative life consequences, diminished self-esteem, and deep shame. No matter your gender, age, race, or sexual orientation, if you are sexually addicted, you are stuck in a cycle of behavior that wreaks havoc on your emotional and physical stability, and on the wellbeing of people around you.

CHAPTER FIVE

LOVE AND ROMANCE ADDICTION IN THE DIGITAL WORLD

I was online constantly—dating websites, smartphone apps, whatever, looking for Mr. Right. Honestly, I joined JDate even though I'm not Jewish. Anything to find the man who could make me feel okay about myself. But the really sad part is I've probably dated tons of great guys. I just get bored with them in a month or so. I keep them around for a while after that, until I find someone else, and then I let them go (if they haven't dumped me already). Now it feels like this cycle might go on forever.

—Shelly, thirty-two, store manager

I date and I date and I date. I'm constantly meeting women on hookup apps and dating apps. Sometimes I even hit them up on social media sites if I see one that looks hot. And every time I meet a new woman I think she's the one. I'm ready to drop everything and jump straight to marriage, but then I start to see the real person behind the cute smile and that ruins it. Why can't one of these women really be as good as she seems when I first meet her and chat her up? Usually, by the fourth or fifth date, whatever that initial spark was that seemed so great is just totally gone.

—Don, fifty-one, antiques dealer

Your Brain on Love

Love may seem ephemeral and indefinable, but it's actually not. In fact, scientists have a pretty good understanding of what romantic love is, how it starts, and how it develops over time. For instance, we know that the brain releases different chemicals at different stages of romantic relationships. In a brand-new relationship, the "first rush of love" incites the same basic neurochemical excitement that drug and sex addicts repetitively exploit—mostly the release of dopamine. Over time as a coupleship grows, this intense attraction fades to a less stimulating but ultimately more meaningful sensation, caused primarily by the release of oxytocin into the brain, resulting in feelings of contentment and satisfaction.

It is thought that these neurochemical releases are in place to foster the initial development of relationships, and then to facilitate people staying together—both of which lead toward reproduction and survival of the human species. The intensity of dopamine pushes us forward toward mating, sexuality, and the production of offspring. Then, later in relationships, after the initial excitement has worn off, oxytocin production increases, helping to cement our feelings of attachment.

Chasing the Dragon

We hope you noticed the following language in the preceding section: *The "first rush of love" incites the same basic neurochemical excitement that drug and sex addicts repetitively exploit.* If you did catch that, then you've probably formulated a relatively accurate idea of what love addiction is all about—repetitively inducing the neurochemical rush that kicks in when we first meet and get to know a potentially special someone.

Nearly everyone can relate to that dopamine-fueled rush of initial attraction and budding romance. This temporary but powerful high is the inspiration for countless songs, poems, novels, paintings, films, greeting cards, and daydreams. It is also a biological imperative, encouraging us to meet and mate and perpetuate the human race. However, most healthy people innately understand that lasting romantic relationships are characterized by much more than neurochemical intensity. In healthy partnerships, true intimacy develops in stages, ultimately resulting in a less intense but infinitely deeper bond. Lasting romantic relationships move—sometimes seamlessly, but more often in fits and starts—from the dopamine-rush tsunami of early attraction to the less intense but equally important oxytocin-fueled stage of intimate bonding.

Love addicts, however, endlessly crave the rush of new love. Instead of growing fonder and closer to a romantic partner as time passes, they become anxious and restless. They seem to think that "love" only exists when dopamine is pumping furiously through their brains. As a result, they are constantly searching for someone new—regardless of whether they've ended the relationship(s) they're already in. Eventually this develops into a pattern of failed romances, each of which begins with passion and fireworks but fizzles and ends badly. Sometimes multiple relationships take place simultaneously, with the highs of one counterbalancing the lows of another.

Love addicts use intense romantic fantasy in the same way and for the same purpose that sex addicts use sex and drug addicts use drugs. A pattern of intense and dramatic but ultimately shallow and meaningless relationships becomes an emotional crutch used to escape stress, emotional discomfort, and even the pain of underlying psychological conditions like depression, anxiety, low self-esteem, attachment deficit disorders, and unresolved early-life or severe adult trauma. Unfortunately, love addicts, like all other addicts, spiral downward in cycles of behavior that reinforce their pre-existing, deeply rooted feelings of shame and self-hatred.

In short, love addicts live in a chaotic world of desperation where romance and sex are peppered with pitfalls, anxiety, and pain. Fearful of isolation and rejection, they endlessly search for that one special person who will make everything okay. In this sense they are similar to porn addicts, who spend countless hours searching for the one perfect image or video that will finally "do it" for them. As love addicts' relationships repeatedly fail, their depression, anxiety, and low self-esteem increase. And, as is the case with all addicts, they typically choose to resolve these painful feelings by engaging in more of the same destructive fantasies and behaviors.

LOVE ADDICTION SIGNS AND SYMPTOMS

There are numerous signs and symptoms of love or romantic addiction. Following are a few of the more common signs in today's tech-driven dating universe:

- Mistaking intense sexual experiences including sexts, webcam sex, and teledildonic sex for love
- Mistaking romantic infatuation (early-relationship texting, video chats, and emails) for love
- Constantly searching for love and romance through dating websites and apps, hookup websites and apps, and social media
- Using sex as a way to find love (agreeing to engage in webcam sex or IRL sex as a way to snare or keep a partner)
- Falling in love with people met online without ever meeting in person
- Difficulty maintaining intimate relationships once the newness and excitement has worn off or after meeting an online love interest in person
- Feeling detached, fearful, or unhappy when in a relationship
- Feeling desperate and alone when not in a relationship
- Using sex—including masturbation to online porn, webcam sex, or virtual sex games—to mask loneliness
- Consistently choosing abusive or emotionally unavailable partners
- Giving emotionally or financially to partners who require a great deal of caretaking but do not or cannot reciprocate
- Using sex, money, seduction, drama, or any other scheme to hook or hold on to a partner
- Missing important family, career, recreational, or social experiences to find, create, or maintain a romantic relationship
- Avoiding sex or relationships both online and IRL for long periods in an attempt to "solve the problem"
- Being unable to leave unhealthy or abusive relationships despite promises to self or others

- Returning to previously unmanageable or painful relationships either online or IRL despite promises to self or others

Not every person who has engaged in these behaviors is a love addict. Indeed, nearly everyone has had his or her judgment skewed by a difficult person or situation at some point. It is when these situations become the norm, lived over and over again to the point of interfering with life goals and daily health functions, that the diagnosis of love addiction is accurately made.

LOVE ADDICTION AND GENDER

Typically, women are more likely than men to self-identify as obsessed with the search for and pursuit of love and the perfect relationship. While men tend to focus on finding and viewing sexual images or participating in objectified sex acts using Internet pornography, virtual sex games, and hookup apps, women tend to engage in relationship-oriented online behaviors—seeking *emotional connection* via text and video chat services, social media, and dating websites and apps. Even when women use the same apps as men, they are likely to refer to them as "dating apps" rather than "sex apps" or "hookup apps."

> *Okay, so it isn't the first time this has happened, but this time I'm pretty certain that I've fallen in love for real with a man I met on Facebook. We haven't met in person yet, but I'm definitely ready, willing, and able to do so. My husband knows about this, and he is desperate to stop me and to save our marriage. Still, I want to leave him, and I have told him so, but the guy I'm in love with hasn't invited me to meet in person yet, and every time I bring it up he changes the subject. My husband is so hurt and angry with me that he told our children about this and they, too, are now furious with me. It feels like my whole life is in turmoil, and the only comfort I feel is when I am online chatting with "him." What can I do?*
>
> —Ellen, forty-five, businesswoman

Of course, love addiction is not the sole purview of women any more than sex addiction is the sole purview of men. Yet much of the time with male love addicts, sexual activity is still a major element.

I nearly lost my wife and kids because of a fantasy. Until recently, I'd spend three to four hours every night on my laptop in the basement, intensely involved in online sex. I kept a daily check-in on my favorite sexual chat rooms, seeing who was there, flirting, hitting on ladies, exchanging photos, and video chatting. I also subscribed to a service where I could order up "models" that would perform live sex in whatever way I requested while I masturbated. Although I never intended to go further than these activities, I felt increasingly drawn to one woman named Cathy who did live online porn.

Over a three-month period, I spent an unbelievable $3,500 on these computer sessions with Cathy. During this time, I increasingly withdrew from my wife and family, and found creative ways to lie about where the money was going. Work also became secondary to this cyber-affair, as I started checking in with Cathy many times throughout the day. I actually began feeling jealous and afraid that she would "get involved" with some other guy online.

The experience became more intense as I started to pursue the "real person" rather than the fantasy. I worked very hard to convince Cathy to tell me her real name and where she lived, and when she finally did, it was the most arousing moment of our entire interaction. She even told me her entire, tragic life story, which hooked me even more. Eventually, convinced that I might be falling in love with her, I requested an in-person meeting, to which she agreed. I made plane and hotel reservations, told my wife a lie about needing to travel for work, and packed my bags. It was only when I heard myself lying to my kids about where Daddy was going that I broke down and realized how out of control I was. Instead of getting on the plane, I called a therapist for help.

—Jeffrey, thirty-six, landscaper

Jeffrey's sad tale illustrates the dynamics that underlie the problem behavior patterns of many male love addicts, in that he used his online relationship as an emotional power contest, trying to get Cathy to need him enough to drop her guard and let him in. The more Cathy seemed to count on and need him, the more arousing the situation became for Jeffrey, the more "love" he felt, and the more he wanted to meet in person. These issues of dependency, potential abandonment, power, sex, and obsession frequently become intermingled for male love addicts, who often are desperately seeking to feel important, wanted, and needed.

Both Ellen and Jeffrey focused their love addiction on a single person. That said, love addicts of both genders often engage in multiple relationships simultaneously, especially when the relationships are entirely digital, keeping each interaction at various stages of development. In this respect, love addicts are sometimes like a computer, with several "windows" open and operating at the same time. This allows them to turn for their fantasy fueled fix to whichever relationship is the most emotionally intense and exciting at that particular moment.

TECHNOLOGY DRIVES THE LOVE ADDICTION BUS

Digital technology fuels love addiction. Even social media sites can be problematic for those predisposed to romantic addiction. Increasingly, love addicts describe social networks like Facebook and Instagram as primary locations in which they conduct their obsessive search for romantic intensity.

> *As a housewife and the mother of two young boys, I take pride in what I do. It has always felt right to me to stay home with my kids, and I have no regrets about that. In fact, I am grateful that we can afford for me to do so. But after our second son was born, I was stuck at home all day with no one to talk to but a baby and a three-year-old, so for some distraction I started going on Facebook to reconnect with friends from high school and family members who'd moved away. Then, out of the blue, I got a poke and an email from a guy I'd never met. At*

first I ignored it, but then, out of curiosity more than anything, I responded. Before I knew it we were video chatting. He was handsome and friendly and very attentive to me, and I liked that. Within a few short weeks I was waiting for my husband to leave each day so I could get back to the computer. These conversations made me feel more alive than I had been in years. Before I knew it, I was deep into a string of online affairs—some with webcam sex, others without it. Now I am completely distracted from parenting, and I've created distance with my husband. I've also lost most of my self-respect. Yet the only thing that seems to make me feel better is going online to search for the very same experiences that make me feel so awful in the first place. I haven't hooked up with anyone in person yet, but I know it's coming, and I'm horribly afraid of what will happen when it does.

—Denise, twenty-seven, housewife and mother

Smartphones, a relatively recent technological development, definitely play into love addicts' compulsive behaviors, as dating sites, porn sites, social media sites, and even virtual sex games can all be accessed via apps, allowing love addiction to be taken on the road. Smartphones further allow for sexting, a favorite acting out tool of nearly every modern love addict. Hookup apps are particularly dangerous for love addicts, allowing them to obsessively engage—anytime, anywhere—in romantic intrigue.

CAUGHT WITH A SEX ADDICT

In their efforts to attract, ensnare, and hold on to a partner, some love addicts shortcut the path to intimacy by quickly agreeing to engage in either cybersex or IRL sex. The outcome is often not what they hoped for. Sometimes love addicts find themselves in a "relationship" with a sex addict who is simply taking advantage of their neediness.

My husband, Ken, and I met on the Internet six years ago. We quickly developed a sexual relationship via webcam. By the time we met in person, six months after first meeting online, we were both in love. I agreed to move halfway across the country to be with him, and we married a short time later. Unfortunately, our actual sex life didn't live up to my expectations. In fact, it was nothing like our online intimacy. Most of the time he had trouble maintaining an erection, and I assumed all the blame because I was very inexperienced and insecure. He was always "too tired" for real sex, and for a long time I didn't know why. I felt lonely and paranoid. He told me to initiate sex more often, but then when I did, he'd often turn me down. I felt so confused.

One day I accidentally walked in on Ken while he was sitting at the computer. He was masturbating on webcam with another woman. Big surprise! It turns out that all along my new husband had been having sex with other women through the Internet. Several times I confronted him and threatened to leave. He always promised to stop, but he never did. Truthfully, I would never have left him—I was too terrified to be alone again. Recently he "fell in love" with another woman on the Internet. Even before he met her in person, he told me he no longer loved me. This has absolutely devastated me. Until I found out about his cybersex activities, I thought this man was the love of my life—my knight in shining armor—despite our sexual problems.

—Judy, thirty-two, day-trader

Judy is a woman who, in her never-ending quest for romance, unknowingly became involved with a sex addict. In her intense desire to please Ken, she willingly had webcam sex with him. She assumed that once they developed a real relationship, he wouldn't need or want the cybersex and would settle into a healthy, loving marriage. This didn't happen, and Judy, based on a desperate fear of being alone, enabled Ken's online obsessions by not following through on her threats to leave. Now, thanks to therapy, she has a clearer understanding of her part in the drama.

Despite the way Ken and I met and how quickly I got attached to him, when I first found him having sex with other women online I made it all his problem and decided he needed to fix it. I had no idea what my part was in the whole situation. Since he left me, I've begun attending Sex and Love Addicts Anonymous and I see a therapist weekly. I'm reading lots of books on addiction, codependency, and love addiction. I now have a better understanding of my role in getting into this relationship in the first place, and I am working on improving my self-esteem. I hope that if I get into another relationship, I will make a better choice.

If your emotional needs cause you to look for a romantic exchange to make yourself feel whole, and if your fear of abandonment makes it difficult for you to trust your own judgment, you are particularly vulnerable to the lure of a fantasy-driven digital romance. Many people, like Judy, initially go online to meet a compatible dating partner and agree to sext or to participate in webcam sex to advance the relationship. Other people, confusing sexual intensity with love, go online specifically seeking sex, believing it will somehow win them love. Unfortunately, when two people meet using digital technology and sex quickly becomes the glue that holds them together, it is unlikely that they will be able to successfully convert the digital relationship to a healthy in-person relationship.

Am I a Love Addict?

The use of digital technology for romantic purposes ranges from casual to addictive. We suggest you take the following quiz to see if you have crossed the line between casual use and addictive use.

Love Addiction Self-Test

Respond "yes" or "no" to each question and then tabulate your "yes" responses.

1. Do you feel detached and/or unhappy when in a relationship, yet desperate and lonely when out of a relationship?

    ☐ YES   ☐ NO

2. Do you avoid relationships and/or sex for long periods of time to "solve the problem" that you seem to have with failed romances?

    ☐ YES   ☐ NO

3. Are you unable to leave unhealthy or abusive relationships despite repeated promises to yourself and/or others?

    ☐ YES   ☐ NO

4. Do you have affairs or intense flirtations and intrigue either online or IRL while already in committed relationships?

    ☐ YES   ☐ NO

5. Do you repeatedly return to previously unmanageable or painful relationships either online or IRL even though you know that nothing is likely to be different this time?

    ☐ YES   ☐ NO

6. Do you repeatedly mistake sex and/or romantic intensity either online or IRL for love?

    ☐ YES   ☐ NO

7. Are you constantly seeking new sexual partners and new romance either online or IRL, even when you're already dating someone?

    ☐ YES   ☐ NO

8. Do you find it difficult to be single, seeking digital or IRL connections simply because you can't stand to be alone?

    ☐ YES   ☐ NO

9. Do you habitually choose partners who are abusive and/or emotionally disinterested and neglectful?

    ☐ YES   ☐ NO

10. Do you use sex, seduction, and intrigue either online or IRL to "hook" or hold on to a partner?

    ☐ YES   ☐ NO

11. Do you seek out sex or romantic intensity either online or IRL as a way to tolerate difficult experiences or emotions?

    ☐ YES   ☐ NO

12. Have you missed out on important family, career, or social experiences in order to search for or maintain a romantic relationship either online or IRL?

    ☐ YES   ☐ NO

13. Do you hide or keep secret certain aspects of your online or IRL dating life?

    ☐ YES   ☐ NO

14. Do you believe that by finding the right relationship partner your life will be complete?

    ☐ YES   ☐ NO

15. Do you feel as if your life lacks meaning (as if you don't matter) when you are not engaged in a romantic relationship either online or IRL?

    ☐ YES   ☐ NO

Total YES answers _____

SCORING:

1 or 2 "yes" answers: You are probably not love addicted.

3 or 4 "yes" answers: You are definitely at risk for love addiction.

5 or more "yes" answers: You are probably a love addict, compulsively using romance in ways that are out of control and negatively impacting your life.

THE NATURE OF ADDICTIVE LOVE

If you are a love addict, your constant search for someone who will both care for and need you likely involves endless intrigue, flirtations, sexual liaisons, affairs, and a lengthy trail of hurt feelings and painful consequences. Without support and direction, you will find few options to resolve these difficult circumstances other than engaging in even more searching, creating over time an escalating cycle of drama, desperation, and loss.

Unlike psychologically healthy people, who seek relationships and sex to enrich their lives, love addicts endlessly search for something outside of themselves to provide the emotional stability they lack within. Similar to drug addicts or alcoholics, love addicts use intensity—in this case the intensity of their arousing emotional and sexual experiences—to "fix" themselves. As a result, they often make poor partner choices. Compatibility becomes based on "how much you want me," "whether you will ever leave me," or "how intense our sex life is," rather than on whether the other person might truly become a peer, friend, and companion.

Addictive love relationships are characterized over time by unhealthy dependency, guilt, and abuse. Convinced of their lack of worth, love addicts will use seduction, control, guilt, and manipulation to attract and hold on to romantic partners. Despairing of this cycle of unhappy affairs, broken relationships, and sexual liaisons, some love addicts have "swearing-off" periods, believing that remaining alone or "just having sex with no love" will solve the problem. When the love addict becomes tired of being alone and re-enters the playing field, those same problems of intimacy and fear reappear.

Of course, anyone can show bad judgment when encountering a difficult person or seductive situation. However, for love addicts, heartache and longing become the norm, lived over and over again in one form or another. If these issues apply to you and you are not actively working toward change or healing, then you are unlikely to learn from your mistakes. It is just so much easier to blame your partners and lovers for being "the problem." Only when the pain of these behaviors and situations becomes greater than the pain and challenges of creating change does the process of genuine healing and recovery begin.

CHAPTER SIX

TO THE CYBERSEX WIDOW AND WIDOWER

My husband's porn use has left me feeling alone, isolated, rejected, and less than a desired woman. Porn hangs a sign on the door that says, "You are not needed. I can take care of myself, thank you very much." I have threatened, manipulated, tried to control, cried, given him the cold shoulder, yelled, tried to be understanding, and even tried to ignore it. But nothing I do seems to change things.

—June, forty-seven, realtor

When our relationship got serious, Jon and I agreed that we weren't going to act like some of the other gay couples we knew. We promised each other to be honest and to have integrity around our sex life. It just never occurred to me that our definitions of fidelity and integrity would differ. I don't want to believe that he is out there having sex with other men, but at this point my confidence has been so shredded by his constant online cruising that I have trouble believing he really loves me. I mean, if he loves me so much, why is he awake until three in the morning chatting up guys on his Grindr app? Why does he even have that app in the first place?

—Alec, thirty, personal trainer

Many modern day, tech-driven sex and love addicts have attractive and willing sexual partners at home—loving people who want not only a sexual relationship but quality time, intimacy, emotional attention, and healthy mutual sharing. Much of the time these men and women struggle to understand their partner's obsession with digital pornography, webcam sex, virtual reality sex games, romantic chat sites, and hookup apps. It just doesn't make sense that their partner would want or need these sexual outlets when they are right there next to them.

Spotting Sex Addiction in a Spouse or Partner

Signs that the tech-driven sexual and romantic activity of your spouse or partner may be a problem in your relationship include:

- They are consistently more involved with pornographic pictures, movies, or online sexual interactions than in being physically intimate and sexual with you.
- They don't want to talk about or consider changing their digital sexual involvement, no matter how upsetting the issue is to you.
- Their consistent reaction to your concern about their online sex, romance, and chatting is anger, denial, blaming, and/or defensiveness.
- They keep secrets or lie to you about their digital sexual involvement or the extent of their use.
- They make promises to you about addressing or changing their sexual behaviors, but fail to keep those promises.
- You feel disrespected, less than, and unimportant because what they are doing online seems to be more of a priority than your relationship.
- They seem unempathetic to how their online activities are affecting you.

THE TRAUMA OF REPEATED INFIDELITY

For people affected by the serial sexual infidelity of an addicted spouse or partner, it's usually not the extramarital sex that causes the deepest pain. What typically hurts committed partners the most is that their trust and belief in the person closest to them has been shattered.

Following are common reactions to learning about a partner's repeated sexual and/or romantic betrayals:

- Out-of-control emotions—excessive emotional reactions, frequent mood shifts, tearfulness, etc.
- Hypervigilance that manifests as "detective work" (checking bills, wallets, computer files, phone apps, browser histories, etc.)
- Obsession about the betrayal
- Efforts to avoid thinking about or discussing the betrayal
- Intrusive thoughts about the betrayal
- Sleeplessness and/or nightmares[1]
- Attempts to combine a series of unrelated events in order to predict future betrayal
- Struggling to focus
- Depression
- Isolation
- Compulsive spending, eating, or exercise
- Addiction (substance and/or behavioral)
- Using sex to keep someone close
- Feeling like you are going crazy

In part, the trauma of sex addiction stems from the fact that while the cheater has obviously known about his or her extracurricular sexual behavior all along and may actually be feeling some relief once the truth is on the table, the betrayed partner is usually blindsided. And even when a spouse is not fully deceived, having had some prior knowledge of the infidelity, he or she is often overwhelmed upon learning the full extent of the addict's behavior. Adding insult to injury, it's not just anyone who caused this pain, loss, and hurt; it's the person they had most counted upon to "have their back." Is it any wonder that partners of sex addicts, upon learning about their loved one's repeated infidelities, often experience acute stress symptoms characteristic of posttraumatic stress disorder.[2]

GASLIGHTING MAKES IT WORSE

"Gaslighting" is a form of psychological abuse where false information is presented to the victim by a spouse or another primary attachment figure, causing the victim to doubt his or her own perceptions, judgments, memories, and even sanity. The term derives from the 1938 stage play *Gaslight* and a pair of film adaptations, one in 1940 and a more famous one in 1944 starring Charles Boyer and Ingrid Bergman. In the 1944 film, Boyer's character convinces his wife (Bergman) that she's imagining things, such as the occasional dimming of the house's gas lights, as part of his ongoing effort to steal her deceased aunt's money and jewels. The gas lights dim whenever he is in the attic, searching for the treasure. Over time, his insistent and persistent lies cause her and others to question her sanity.

Despite the somewhat outlandish plot of *Gaslight*, denying someone's intuitive sense of reality is actually a relatively common form of abuse and manipulation.[3] Therapists who treat sex addicts and their betrayed spouses hear about this sort of thing all the time. Typically, sex addicts deny their betrayed partners' intuition and reality for years, continually insisting that they are not cheating, that they really did need to stay at work until midnight, that they are not being indifferent or distant, and that the worried spouse is just being paranoid, mistrustful, and unfair. Some will devalue their spouse to justify their sexual behaviors calling them overweight, old, or some other derogatory term to protect their continued acting out. In this way betrayed partners are made to feel as if they are the problem. Over time, they often lose faith in their ability to accurately perceive reality, and they start to blame themselves for what they are thinking and feeling.

The lies that sex addicts intentionally perpetrate upon their loved ones so they can continue their behaviors without interference are absolutely relentless. And usually they are just plausible enough to *possibly* be true.

And when gaslighting continues over a long enough period of time, victims learn to doubt and dismiss their feelings and intuition, and to believe the addict's lies and manipulative defenses. When this happens, the victims take on responsibility for the problems in their relationship, even though it's the addict who is causing the vast majority of those problems.

Sadly, even emotionally healthy people are vulnerable to gaslighting, primarily because it occurs slowly and gradually over time. It's a bit like the fable that says you can place a frog in a pot of lukewarm water and slowly bring it to a boil without the frog jumping out. Because the temperature rises so gradually, the frog never even realizes it's being cooked. This is the psychological abuse that sex addicts *intentionally inflict* upon their spouses and partners—all so they can continue their addiction unabated.

How Can You Be Mad at Me When It's Not Even Real Sex?

As traumatic as cybersex addiction is to betrayed spouses and partners, the addicts themselves rarely see things that way—blithely justifying, minimizing, and flat-out denying the problematic nature of their behavior. A few of the statements that cybersex addicts commonly drop on their partners include:

- I've never even met him (or her) in person, so it's not cheating.
- It's your fault for walking in on me while I'm online. I deserve some privacy.
- It's totally digital. They're not even real people to me.
- Webcam sex is the same as porn, and everybody looks at porn at least occasionally.
- All men (or women) do this. It's perfectly normal to engage in a little bit of online fantasy.
- My dad kept a stack of *Playboy* magazines in the closet and my mom never complained, so why are you so worked up about my porn stash?
- You're not a man (or a woman), so you can't understand.

- I will never hook up with him (or her) in person, so what's the big deal?
- This is a total fantasy, a game. I don't know their last names or anything about their lives.
- I'm only playing around with people who are thousands of miles away, so it's not like I'm having an affair.
- I haven't had actual sex with a single other person.
- How can you say I'm cheating when I've never even touched another person sexually?

The truth is that most cybersex addicts develop a "belief" that digital sexual activity somehow doesn't count as cheating thereby denying how their spouses and partners typically feel.

In an attempt to understand the emotional reactions of people affected by tech-driven sexual infidelity, we created an online survey, receiving and analyzing the responses of twenty-nine women and five men who were partners to a sex addict. As part of the survey, we asked the betrayed partners to describe how the addict's behaviors affected them emotionally, intellectually, physically, and spiritually.[4] Not surprisingly, almost all of the respondents reported that their partner's online activities were every bit as hurtful and consequential as in-person cheating. The most common complaints were loss of trust, loss of self-esteem, stress and anxiety brought on by the cumulative effect of lying/gaslighting, and diminishment of the sexual relationship.

Loss of Trust

A few years ago, partners of cybersex addicts could find out pretty much everything the addict was up to by checking the browser history on the addict's computer. Nowadays, with smartphones and other digital devices, it's much harder to know what's actually happening. For starters, most of these devices don't keep the same type of "history" that computers do, so there is less to search for. Plus, many apps are designed to help cheaters cover their tracks—disguising icons, automatically deleting sexts, etc. As a result, partners of cybersex addicts have difficulty knowing if they have been told the whole truth about the addict's behaviors. This was readily apparent in our survey, with less than one-third of the betrayed partners saying they were confident they knew the full truth. Following is a sampling of what betrayed spouses told us:

> *I can't trust him, and now I struggle to trust others in my life. I want to be angry, yet I find myself hurt. I am heartbroken, depressed at times, frustrated, and confused.*

> *Trust has been shattered beyond belief.*

> *I think it is a fantasy to expect fully restored trust. For me, as time goes by and his behavior now continues to match his words, I trust him more. Now my motto is "Trust, but verify."*

Loss of Self-Esteem

It's difficult to not take it personally when it feels as if your mate has lost sexual interest in you, or is comparing your body to the highly idealized porn found online. Without a doubt, fears about "measuring up" to digital partners can be incredibly damaging to a cheated-on partner's self-image, self-confidence, and self-esteem. In our survey betrayed spouses said:

> *Fantasy sex leaves practically nothing to be desired when compared with the all-too-human and flawed spouse.*

> *Now I feel unattractive and ugly. I'm always wondering what's wrong with me that he needs to go online all the time. I can't sleep or concentrate. I'm missing out on life's happiness, and I'm worried and scared all the time.*

> *When he closes his eyes when we are together, what is he thinking about? The babe in the movie? Is he happy with my body? Is he grossed out?*

Stress and Anxiety Brought on by the
Cumulative Effect of Lying/Gaslighting

Typically, sex addicts lie about what they are doing, covering up their behavior with semi-plausible mistruths. Nevertheless, they expect their spouse to believe what they are saying. And, as we have long known from work with abused children, being made to feel wrong when you are right is a solid foundation for stress and anxiety. Sadly, after a sex addict's behavior is uncovered and he or she promises to stop acting out, the problematic behaviors usually continue, often with the lying and secrecy bumped up a notch. And even when the behaviors do stop, there is disclosure to deal with. Sex addicts are notorious for admitting part but not all of what they've done. Then, later, when more about their past leaks out, the betrayed partner is traumatized yet again—not so much by the cheating, but by the lying and the continued keeping of secrets. Constantly worrying about what you haven't heard yet can be extremely stressful. In our survey betrayed spouses said:

> *The lies he told me concerning his whereabouts, while looking me straight in the eye, hurt worse than his out-of-control sexual behavior.*

> *How could I trust or believe him when he would continually lie to me even when I caught him in the act? Then he would blame me and shame me for being "too prudish." He would try to make me feel guilty, and he often succeeded.*

> *The denial of my reality resulted in my believing I was crazy. I became over the top with snooping, spying, trying to control the addiction, and thinking if I just found out about everything, then I could stop it. It caused complete erosion of my self-esteem, boundaries, and sense of self.*

Diminishment of the Sexual Relationship

Marital problems are a given among couples when one of the partners is a sex or love addict. In some cases, the problems result from the sex addict's decreased interest in sex with the same old partner. In others, it is primarily the betrayed spouse who loses interest because he or she feels insecure, unwanted, or unattractive. In some cases, neither partner wants sex with the other. In fact, our survey found that both members of the couple remained interested in having sex with each other only about 30 percent of the time.

Interestingly, several of the cheated-on spouses reported extramarital affairs of their own, undertaken either to shore up their self-esteem or to exact revenge. Others reported engaging in sexual activities with the sex addict that they did not enjoy or even found distasteful, all to "appease" and "win back" the sex addict's intimate attention. In our survey betrayed spouses said:

> *Sometimes I would "take sex" from him because I felt he owed me that much. But basically any sex that occurred was unsatisfying and left me feeling angry, unwanted, unattractive, and used. Now I don't feel anything when we are sexual. I can no longer reach orgasm with him. I'm always afraid that any sexual attention he gives me is because he's been viewing porn or talking sexual with someone online. It makes it hard to just enjoy the here and now with him.*

> *At first we had sex more than ever, as I desperately tried to prove myself. But then sex with her made me sick. I'd get strong pictures of what she did and lusted after, and then I'd get repelled and feel bad. I used to see sex as a very intimate, loving thing. We always had a lot of sex and I felt we were intimate. Since I found out my wife was not on the same page, though, I can't be intimate or vulnerable.*

> *I realize now that many of the things he liked and requested when we made love were re-creations of images he had viewed online. He is no longer able to be intimate. He objectifies me, other women, and girls on the street. When we go out, it's like his head is on a swivel, staring at every woman who goes by. When we're together in bed, he fantasizes about the women he's seen online and imagines that he's having sex with one of them. I know he does; I can feel it. I have been humiliated, used, betrayed, lied to, and misled. It's almost impossible to let him touch me without feeling really yucky. I tried to continue being sexual*

with him initially. In fact, I tried being more sexual, to compete better with the porn girls, but I couldn't do it. Now we've stopped having sex altogether.

IF IT'S A SECRET, THEN IT'S CHEATING

One of the things our survey made abundantly clear was that, when it comes to the negative effects of sexual infidelity, tech-sex and IRL sex are no different. Either form of extramarital sexual activity is a betrayal of relationship trust. The lying and emotional unavailability of a cybersex addict who "only" engages in porn and masturbation feels the same to the betrayed partner as when an addict has a real world affair. No matter what, the tech-sex widows and widowers we talked to felt betrayed, devalued, deceived, "less than," and abandoned—the same as with an in-the-flesh affair. Here are some reflections these men and women shared with us:

> *He did have affairs, although not physical ones. He had affairs of the mind that to me were as much a violation as if he'd actually had a physical affair with someone. He committed adultery just the same as if he had another real partner. Moreover, in a sense I feel that having an affair of the mind is worse than having an actual partner. My husband can, at any time, have an "affair" without leaving the house or seeing another human being.*

> *I may not be getting a disease from him, but I'm not getting anything else either!*

> *My husband is using sexual energy that should be used with me. The person on the other end of that computer is live and is participating in a sexual activity with him. They are doing it together and responding to each other. To engage in an interactive sexual encounter means that you are being sexual with another person, and that is cheating.*

Of the people we surveyed, 40 percent said their cybersex addicted partner had also engaged in at least one instance of in-the-flesh infidelity.

These people were able to compare how they felt about their partner's online activities versus how they felt about the offline affairs. In general, they experienced the same level and caliber of hurt.

My husband has actually cheated on me with a real partner, and it feels no different! The online "safe" cheating feels to me just as dirty and filthy as the "real-life" cheating.

HOW ABOUT MORE SEX AT HOME?

Without fully understanding the escapist nature of sexual addiction, it might be easy to assume that a person's compulsive sexual activity simply means that he or she is not getting enough "good loving" at home. This misguided assumption makes it harder for most significant others to reach out for help, fearing that they will be blamed or judged for "not keeping him (or her) satisfied." It is still a common societal belief that lots of really good sex at home will keep a spouse from straying. However, this is simply not the case. In reality, the allure of illicit sex with an unfamiliar partner can easily survive even abundant sex at home.

In an attempt to control an out-of-control situation, betrayed partners will sometimes try to increase the frequency of sexual activities in their relationship or agree to participate in sexual activities they find uncomfortable or even offensive. This is much like the spouses and partners of alcoholics and drug addicts who resort to drinking and using with the addict in an attempt to "keep up" and therefore stay connected. It just doesn't work, because that's not what the addiction is all about.

Some partners of sex addicts actually try joining the addict in cybersex activities. They usually discover that their involvement does not prevent the addict from continuing with his or her problematic behavior.

My husband is a minister who was stationed overseas for a year. We chatted daily, but never sexually. One day he admitted to me that he'd been involved in cybersex activities with other women online. He said it had nothing to do with us and that it didn't affect his feelings for me. But I felt cheated. Why wouldn't he ask me to have cybersex? I guessed it was because he thought I was too old-fashioned, so I told him I was willing to try it with him. I wasn't comfortable with it, but I thought I could "rescue" him. We began a long-distance online sexual relationship. Much to my horror, he never quit with the anonymous partners. Instead he lumped me in with all the online whores. When he returned, he continued his cybersex even though we were reunited. We're still together, but his online activities have really come between us.

—Kim, fifty-two, housewife

Attempts to solve a partner's cybersex addiction problem by providing more real world or even virtual sex are usually ineffective and short-lived. And it's common for spouses who have participated in activities they found uncomfortable to feel shame and anger later, even though what they attempted was a natural and fairly typical response.

Dealing with Betrayal

Partners of sex addicts are likely to experience shame, doubt, loss of self-esteem, betrayal, self-blame, a worsening of their sex life, depression, and anger. They are then likely to embark on a course of action that may include ongoing detective work, bargaining with the cybersex user, and attempting to control the behavior.

Emotional reactions to a cybersex addict's lies and behaviors can range from feelings of devastation and rage to feelings of betrayal and abandonment. Sometimes the cheated-on partner's behaviors are described as codependent or co-addicted. For instance, in our survey many partners reported checking the addict's computer, smartphone, and other devices because of their suspicions. This propensity for "snooping behaviors" has been interpreted as an unhealthy desire to control the addict. Instead, these actions represent the partner's attempt to feel safe in an unsafe environment, the partner's need to know more detailed information in order to understand the past and avoid future pain, and the partner's need to feel as if he or she has some control over an out-of-control situation.

Recently, clinicians have begun to recognize that the discovery of sexual or romantic betrayal by a long-term partner typically evokes a profound and recurring form of psychological trauma, as broken relationship trust can lead a betrayed partner to have feelings similar to those experienced when losing an important job, a child, or a home.[5] The subsequent behaviors of partners who experience this relational betrayal are consistent with a perfectly normal trauma response—especially when there is repeated dishonesty by a sexually addicted mate, who often denies the spouse's concerns, gut reactions, and instincts. Sometimes the cheated-on spouse's emotions and reactions feel and look a little crazy, even though they are fairly normal when examined in context.[6] These emotions and responses may include the following:

- Feeling as if you are not a worthwhile or lovable person
- Doubting your own sexual attractiveness
- Neglecting your own needs and desires while focusing on others' needs and desires
- Denying the seriousness of problems in your life
- Feeling responsible for someone else's behavior
- Setting boundaries or agreements but not following through with the stated consequences; for example, saying you will leave if he/she cheats again, but not following through when he/she does
- Accepting sexual attention as a substitute for relational intimacy
- Making excuses for the addict's behavior
- Keeping secrets about the addict's behavior
- Failing to confront the addict about his/her behaviors for fear of abandonment
- Remaining too long in harmful situations
- Engaging in "detective work" in an attempt to know and therefore control everything that is happening
- Becoming tearful for no apparent reason
- Shifting from happy to sad to angry very quickly, sometimes for no apparent reason

Self-care for Partners

Typically, partners of sex addicts have lost trust not only in their addicted partner, but in themselves. Often they have been so heavily invested in their relationship that when given a choice between believing their own instincts and believing a lie told to them by the addict, they opt for the lie. This is why partners of sex and love addicts are often the last to know about the sex addict's behavior, even when there have been many clues along the way. As such, betrayed partners, and the relationship as a whole, nearly always benefit when they make it a priority to work on themselves.

Although many partners rightly feel that they didn't create the problem and in fact have been victimized, a great deal of growth can still be achieved by seeking help. Counseling and self-help groups can result in improved self-esteem, less reactivity, and increased willingness to again risk vulnerability with the addict. This work also helps betrayed people learn to trust their own perceptions and judgment, therefore empowering them. Once they learn to rely on their gut feelings to inform them that something is wrong, they are more likely to once again risk trusting, and less likely to be taken advantage of.

For partners, an important aspect of healing from sexual betrayal is learning to pay attention to their own gut reactions. When they trust themselves, using their own reactions as a guide to their responses, the world no longer seems so unpredictable. They feel in greater control of their world and they have less of a need to control others. They will also be in a better position to make choices about their life, including whether they want to stay in the relationship (as most betrayed partners of sex addicts choose to do). One study asked the partners of recovering sex addicts to describe why they decided to stay in their relationship and what would cause them to leave.[7] Here are some of the reasons that betrayed spouses gave for continuing their relationship:

- The value of the relationship—a belief that we can work through this and the relationship overall is worth it
- Practical considerations—finances and/or children

- The addict's commitment to change—he or she has been active in Twelve Step groups and has been doing serious therapy
- Hope or faith—the belief that a better marriage is coming
- A feeling/belief that we share much more than this tragedy—kids, friends, family, home, etc.
- A healthy unwillingness to give up or change "my personal/financial life" and/or "my children's life/home"

And here are the circumstances that would cause the partners to leave the relationship:

- A relapse in sexual recovery
- Dishonesty—discovery that the addict is again lying
- Cessation of recovery work by the addict

Whether partners choose to remain in their relationship with a sex addict or to end it, learning to really listen to their gut and trust themselves is a prerequisite for negotiating the world with confidence and faith. Later in this book we will describe how couples can work together to rebuild trust and improve their relationship. In the next chapter, we'll see how these issues can affect whole families.

CHAPTER SEVEN

KIDS, FAMILY LIFE, AND CYBERSEX ADDICTION

When I found out my mom was seeing other people, I felt really confused. I thought, "Why is she married to my dad if she wants to have all of these affairs?" And then I started to worry about what was going to happen to our family. I couldn't understand why my dad would stay with her, but I also didn't want him to walk out. One minute I was really angry with my mom, and then the next minute I was really angry with my dad for putting up with it. And then I'd get angry with myself and I don't even know why. Most of the time I don't know what to feel, and I just want to hide in my room with the door locked so I don't have to deal with it or even think about it.

—Mariah, thirteen

I have yelled at my husband repeatedly about his porn addiction, even threatening to leave him, and I've told him time and time again that our sons would find out what he was doing. And now they have. They're only fifteen, ten, and eight, but they've all found his porn stash on his laptop, and I know the oldest two have started searching for porn on their own. Our oldest boy I can maybe understand, but ten is too young. He hasn't even hit puberty. And what about my little one? If his older brothers are into it, he's not far behind. But it's my eldest son I'm most worried about. He spends almost as much time locked in his room as his dad spends locked in his study. His grades are going down, and now he says he doesn't want to play sports this year. I can't seem to make my husband stop what he's doing, and me telling the boys that looking at this stuff is not appropriate or okay sounds pretty lame to them when their dad does it all the time.

—Portia, thirty-nine, artist

I started looking at and masturbating to porn a few years ago. At first it got me more interested in girls at school, but now they don't do anything for me at all. I'm worried that my sex life is over before it even started. I mean, I'm only fifteen and still a virgin. I went out on a double date a couple of weeks ago with a friend of mine, and all I could think about was, "When will this date end so I can get home to my laptop?"

—Dashiell, fifteen

Children are affected in two main ways by sex and love addiction. First, active addiction in a parent changes the family dynamics in ways that create trauma and confusion in kids' lives. Second, a child's own sexual compulsivity can derail his or her development, leading to problems at school and at home, disintegrating friendships, a loss of interest in real world romantic interactions, and more. This chapter examines young people and sexual addiction, starting with the negative effects brought on by a parent's hypersexual activity and concluding with the problems that arise when kids and teens are compulsively sexual themselves.

When Mom or Dad Is an Addict

A primary caretaker addicted to sex, drugs, food, gambling, spending, or anything else does not treat his or her family as a major life priority. Addiction, no matter the form, nearly always takes precedence over everything else in life—including family. If a cybersex addicted father must choose between mutual masturbation via webcam and helping with his son's math homework, the siren song of his laptop will likely win out. If a romance addicted mother is shopping with her daughter and a hot new love interest hits her up on Ashley Madison, the shopping excursion will almost certainly be cut short. And whatever lame explanations are given, the message the child receives is clear: "You are not very important."

The simple truth is sexual and romantic acting out takes time and focus away from active and involved parenting. Yes, many parents who are sex and love addicts will at least go through the motions of being a mom or dad, but they do so without the emotional investment that helps children feel bonded and attached. Sometimes the spouses of sex and love addicts also become less available for parenting and healthy family attachment, thanks to their preoccupation with the addicted partner's sexual and romantic activities. Plus, it is not unusual for relationships decimated by sex or love addiction to end in divorce. Nowadays, of course, divorce is much more common and therefore much less stigmatizing than it once was, but that doesn't mean it's not still highly traumatic for children. At best, these kids lose the presence of a parent in the home and the power and emotional comfort of a "united front" when it comes to parenting decisions. And even if the marriage survives, children still suffer—witnessing arguments and deep emotional conflict, and living with excessive stress in the home.

WHEN KIDS DISCOVER A PARENT'S "STASH"

In some cases, children actually stumble upon and view pornography, sexts, romantic profiles, sexualized chat sessions, and other material on a parent's laptop, smartphone, or other digital device. And do kids really want to know that one of their parents is looking at explicit porn or cheating on the other parent? Even worse, kids—who in general are not great respecters of privacy—have a tendency to walk in on a cybersex addicted parent who is masturbating to pornography or engaging in webcam sex. This is a nightmare scenario for everyone involved.

If an adult in the home is heavily involved with cybersex, it is just plain unrealistic to expect that children and teenagers will not learn about this, want to find out more about it, and access online sexual material themselves. There is not much that parents who are active cybersex addicts can do about this until they address their own problems with sexuality.

In the same way that admonitions to not drink made by a parent who is an active alcoholic are likely to fall upon deaf ears, lectures about the evils of porn use are likely to be ignored if they are given by a parent who is spending hours online viewing porn. A parent with an active addiction simply has no credibility, and the only way that he or she is going to gain any credibility is by admitting there is a problem and seeking help. This means that the first step to having a healthy, non-addicted family is for parents to own and actively deal with their own problems.

> *I discovered about a year ago that my father is a sex addict. I guess it's been an issue for a long time, but I didn't know about it until I borrowed his iPhone and found all sorts of nasty stuff on it. And now I just found out that he didn't get laid off from work; he got fired because he was looking at porn on a company-owned computer. I guess he had a couple of warnings about it, but he didn't listen, and now he's out of a job and we're totally broke. Plus, I'm afraid that I'll be a sex addict, too. I have a girlfriend and I think about sex stuff a lot. But now I don't know if I even want to kiss her because if I get started, I might go off the deep end and ruin everything just like my dad. I'm really confused, and I'm really angry with both of my parents, and I don't know what to do.*
>
> —Roberto, twelve

Not surprisingly, upon discovering a father's porn collection, a mother's online affair, or either parent masturbating at the computer, a child experiences a great deal of emotional turmoil. Depending on the child's age, these emotions may include the following:

- Psychological trauma
- Shock at the parent's behavior
- Worries about what this means for the parents' relationship and the family's future
- Confusion and misunderstanding, possibly mixed with interest and arousal

- Embarrassment at having to face the fact that a parent is sexual
- Anger that one parent is betraying the other
- A sense of loss that mom or dad is not the idealized person the child may have thought
- Fears that the marriage will end and one parent will leave
- A sense of power at holding an important family secret
- Curiosity to learn more about what's available online

It is essential that kids are not left alone with their confusing thoughts and feelings. They absolutely must have an outlet where they can openly and honestly discuss what they've encountered and what they are now experiencing—without shame, embarrassment, or fear of judgment.

COMMUNICATING WITH KIDS ABOUT A PARENT'S SEX OR LOVE ADDICTION

When there's a crisis in the family and the particulars of that problem are unknown to their children, parents are not required to explain every detail to them. However, even very young children are highly sensitive to both parental moods and interactions. In those families where children are too young to understand the specific details of their parents' problems, a more general approach is needed (but the talk has to be held nonetheless). By saying general things like, "Mom and dad are very angry at each other, but this is not your fault, we both love you very much and are doing our best. Do you have any questions?" a parent is always making a better choice than by saying nothing at all.

It is more harmful to children when they are told things like, "These are mom and dad's problems, not yours," or worse, "Everything is fine, don't worry," when clearly everything does not feel fine to them. Talking to kids of all ages about their parent's emotional and addictive problems is a situation by situation and family by family decision and process (one best guided by a family therapy professional). Even older children and teens may be best off not hearing specific details related to adult parental addictions, infidelity, and sexuality.

A general rule for what to tell children who are unaware of parental challenges is to acknowledge that there is a problem, reassuring them that it is not their fault, and letting them know that you will keep them in the loop and will answer any questions. In this way children who feel family tensions and hear arguments can better tolerate the situation with less fear and isolation.

Children of sex addicts who have inadvertently learned about a parent's sexual or romantic activities also need to have their feelings validated, whatever those feelings may be, and to hear an explanation from one or both parents. Children who have discovered a parent's problem with sex or love addiction, perhaps because of an impending divorce or constant parental bickering, need and deserve the same validation and explanation. In all cases, any information given to the child must be age appropriate and only shared to benefit the child, never as a means of venting infidelity-related rage to the child. You can read more about talking with children in two recent books: *Disclosing Secrets: An Addict's Guide to When, to Whom, and How to Reveal* and *Surviving Disclosure: A Partner's Guide for Healing the Betrayal of Intimate Trust.*

Common questions asked by kids when faced with a parent's sex addiction include the following:

- Preteen children may want to know: Am I normal? Did someone do something bad by looking at this? What will happen to me if you get divorced?
- Teens want to know: How could you do this to mom/dad/the family? How does this specifically relate to me? If you do this stuff, am I going to do it, too?
- Children of all ages want to know that the parents will handle the situation and these issues will be talked about and worked through, not just left hanging.

No matter what, both parents need to understand that it is harmful for kids when one of them attempts to form an alliance with a child against the other, or for either parent to turn a child into a confidant. In fact, it is amazingly destructive to a child for an angry parent, feeling violated by a spouse's extramarital activity, to share details about these issues with the child. By nature, children lack the emotional resources to understand the problem and they should not be in this sort of emotionally dependent intimate partnership with anyone, let alone a parent. There is even a name for this sort of behavior: covert incest. And yes, covert incest can be every bit as damaging as overt incest.[1]

KIDS AND CHANGING CULTURAL NORMS

At one time parents were terrified that television would rot the minds of young people or evoke violent behavior. Adults saw their kids wasting hours in front of the television (time that previous generations of young people spent outdoors or reading books or engaging in some other fun or productive activity) and they naturally worried about the effects this might have. There were even congressional hearings on the matter with many parents and childcare professionals seeking to implement drastic restrictions or even to eliminate television entirely. Rock and roll elicited a similar reaction. But while many adults of the era were screaming "The sky is falling," young people simply adjusted to the changing times. Instead of being turned into mindless zombies, they integrated television and rock music into their lives in healthy, life affirming ways. Sure, a few of them went overboard and experienced negative consequences as a result, but for the most part these were the kids who were destined, thanks to genetics or environmental factors, to struggle anyway. Television and rock music merely provided a new outlet for this.

Today we're seeing a similar phenomenon with the Internet. Many adults fear the long-term effects of kids' seemingly 24/7 involvement with digital devices. Of course, as with previous generations, these fears are distorted by personal experience and the lens of their own time, place, and culture. In other words, most adults are generationally biased, naturally thinking that the way they did it (and still do it) is the best (and maybe the only) way to do it. As such, their opinions are based more on fear of the unknown than actual facts.

Unsurprisingly, these tech-related fears are usually compounded when it comes to sexual activity. Even though most adults were somewhat sexual (or at least sexually curious) during their adolescence, they seem to think their children should not be. Thus, digital porn, sexting, online hookups, and other digital sexual behaviors often cause serious consternation among adults. However, kids are simply experimenting with sex as they always have; they're just doing it in new venues with somewhat different social mores. As such, parents need to understand that even though a teen girl snapping a topless picture of herself and giving it to her boyfriend would have been shocking twenty years ago, today, thanks to the ease with which this can occur, this behavior is relatively common and does not necessarily indicate an emotional or psychological issue. Yes, it's still a display of bad judgment, but since when do we expect adolescents to always make good decisions?

In short, the vast majority of teenagers who experiment with digital sexuality are not sexually addicted. Cultural norms change and we adapt. That's human cultural evolution. In terms of addiction and sexual content online, the simple truth is teens naturally experiment with sexual fantasy and behaviors. In today's world that experimentation is usually facilitated by digital technology. Sometimes kids even do this in problematic ways with negative consequences. *But this does not mean they're addicted.* In reality, most young people are able to experiment with porn, video chat, friend finder apps, and other sexnologies without becoming compulsive.

Kids and Digital Sexuality

At one time, if a kid wanted to look at porn, it took quite a lot of effort. To see some naked pictures, that kid or one of his friends would have to locate and surreptitiously raid his father's or an older brother's stash of magazines, steal a *Playboy* from a local gas station, or find some discarded porn in a dumpster. The options were limited, and kids mostly played sneak-a-peek with whatever sexy pictures they could find. As a result, a mere twenty-five years ago the odds of a suburban teenager getting hooked on porn were roughly the same as that same kid getting hooked on heroin—close to zero. Lack of access prevented addiction.

Those days are long gone. In the digital age, hardcore pornography is widely and instantly accessible to anyone who goes looking for it. So if a teen is curious about sex—and most are—all he or she needs to do is find a porn site, click a button that says "Yes I'm eighteen," and he or she is in. There is no need to flash a driver's license as proof of age, nor is there a need to borrow a parent's credit card for payment, as nowadays most porn is available free of charge.

Depending on your point of view, this may or may not be alarming. If you are a sixteen-year-old boy in the throes of adolescence, this might sound just fine and "Thank you, Internet!" But if you are the parent of that same young man, maybe it's not so great—especially if he is looking at porn several hours per night, not doing his homework, and losing interest in real world dating. And if that description sounds a lot like porn addiction, it should. As much as we'd like to think that kids can't possibly be cybersex addicts, they can be. After all, today's kids have as much access to highly stimulating sexual imagery, activity, and potential partners as their parents. And like their parents, some of them are vulnerable to addiction.

For the most part, porn addiction develops in young people in the same basic ways as any other addiction—primarily in at-risk kids who are vulnerable thanks to genetics and/or early-life emotional abuse, physical abuse, sexual abuse, neglect, and family dysfunction. Like adult cybersex addicts, these kids learn to abuse porn as a way to numb, thereby temporarily avoiding the experience of stress, emotional discomfort, and the pain of underlying psychological conditions like depression, anxiety, unresolved trauma, and low self-esteem.

BEYOND PORN

There's much more than just 'simple porn' for adolescents to deal with. Other digitally driven sexual temptations include sexting, using webcams for mutual masturbation, using dating sites and adult friend finder apps like Tinder to meet and hook up in-person with others who are looking for sex, playing virtual sex games, purchasing and using sex toys, and more. In reality, any sexnology that's available to an adult is also available to a kid.

Consider Magdalena, a 16-year-old girl latchkey high school girl who regularly logs on to Skout and Tinder. On her Tinder profile she lies by saying that she's a 20-year-old college student at a local university, who's seeking NSA (no strings attached) sexual encounters. She lists the sex acts she likes to perform and she has the pictures to prove it. For more than a year she's been hooking up at least once per week after school with guys of all ages for anonymous sexual encounters. The men she meets often give her gifts or money which makes her feel special. Despite taking precautions, she's had to visit the free clinic on three different occasions over the past year related to an STD. To date, her parents are unaware of her illicit sexual activity as she told them she's in a late afternoon study group.

Magdalena has found a way to feel like she's getting the attention and love she lacks at home. And she finds it via geo-located male sex partners. To the men it appears that she's a fun college student who is eager for some adult entertainment. And while many emotionally vulnerable kids have sought out adult sexuality as a means of feeling connected or worthwhile in the past, current technology just makes it all so much easier and faster to find sex, keep it hidden, and then simply drift from encounter to encounter.

SPOTTING SEXUAL ADDICTION IN KIDS

Unfortunately, we don't have a legitimate criteria-based diagnosis for sex addiction in children and adolescents. But that doesn't mean problematic sexual behaviors don't exist in kids. There isn't a week that goes by when the authors of this book don't get at least a few calls or emails from people seeking treatment for teens who are sexually acting out in an abusive or compulsive way. And that last bit—abusive or compulsive—is the difference between healthy behavior and a behavioral disorder. Common warning signs that an adolescent may be experiencing problems around compulsive sexual behavior include the following:

- A demonstrated lack of empathy toward other people involved either directly or indirectly in the child's sexual behavior
- Viewing or masturbating to pornography or online chats for multiple hours per day or night
- Decreased interest in or declining performance in school and extracurricular activities
- Diminished interest in and diminished ability to socialize with peers, often manifested by loss of friends
- Excessive interest or a total lack of interest in typical adolescent dating activities
- Secretive computer and smartphone usage—erasing browser histories, setting password protections on devices, etc.
- Lying to parents or others about the nature or the amount of sexual or romantic activities
- Sexual aggression, incest, or age-inappropriate relationships
- Secrecy in general, such as spending large amounts of time alone in a room with the door locked
- Getting into cigarettes, alcohol, or drugs
- Sexual behavior involving alcohol or other drug use
- Unexplained mood swings
- Poor self-care, including lack of exercise, showers, or grooming

Consider Alex, a sixteen-year-old high school student who started looking at online porn when he was ten. Alex has locked himself in his room every evening for more than a year, spending two to three hours each night looking at porn. His grades have dipped because he rarely does much homework or studies for examinations. The girls who once were interested in him now leave him alone. At school he masturbates in a bathroom stall to videos stored on his iPad. After school he sneaks off to meet with strangers for anonymous sex. Most of the time they either don't let him in or they kick him out after a short time, but he still goes. In the past six months school administrators have repeatedly suggested to his parents that he has a problem with alcohol or drugs, little suspecting his real issue.

Alex started seeing a therapist a month ago after his mother searched his computer, found a portion of the thousands of hardcore images and videos he'd downloaded, and confronted him. So far, Alex is resistant to change, though he does accept that his life has degenerated to the point where he has no friends left and he'll be lucky to get into college.

CONSEQUENCES OF SEXUAL ADDICTION IN OUR YOUTH

When adolescents engage in sexual behavior compulsively and addictively, their social, emotional, and psychological growth can be stunted. These kids tend to miss important growth milestones of adolescence and, as a result, they may struggle as adults with dating, developing relationships, and forming true intimacy. And, needless to say, adolescent sex addicts also suffer many of the same consequences as adult sex addicts, such as:

- Social isolation, loneliness
- Depression
- Anxiety
- Relationship problems with girlfriends/boyfriends, parents, teachers, and other adults
- Declining performance in school
- Hours, sometimes days, lost to sexual fantasy, porn use, masturbation, and other sexual behaviors
- Physical harm to genitalia caused by excessive masturbation
- Drug and alcohol use/abuse/addiction in conjunction with sexual acting out
- Sexually transmitted diseases
- Risks related to anonymous hook-ups

Other Online Challenges

With youngsters, digitally driven problems are hardly limited to porn addiction and other forms of sexual addiction. Young people must also deal with cyberbullying, sexting, social media obsession, and stranger danger.

- **Cyberbullying:** This is the deliberate, repeated, and hostile use of digital technology to harm other people. This new form of childhood torture is nearly always perpetrated by other kids via texts and social media, which makes it very hard to monitor and police. And the results can be devastating. In 2010, a fifteen-year old Massachusetts girl, Phoebe Prince, hanged herself after being bullied and humiliated on social media for nearly three months by multiple students at her high school.[2] Since that time, numerous other cyberbullying suicides have occurred. And those are just the incidents we hear about! Nobody knows how many kids simply suffer this sort of abuse in silence.

- **Sexting:** Now that computers and smartphones have built-in digital cameras and webcams, it is incredibly easy to impulsively take a provocative selfie and send it to another person. Unfortunately, once that image is sent, the child loses all control over it; the recipient may keep it private, forward it to others, or post it online for public viewing. For teens, sexted images are redefining what it means to have a bad breakup, as resentful former boyfriends or girlfriends can send or post an ex's nude image pretty much anywhere, anytime.

- **Social media obsession:** Children and adults alike are vulnerable to social media obsession, where the number of friends or followers you have is a status symbol, and the ways in which your lovingly constructed posts and adorable selfies are responded to or ignored correlate directly to your waxing and waning self-esteem. Those obsessed with social media often choose to bypass real world relationships, recreation, and social engagement for their online life.

- **Stranger danger:** The vast majority of online interactions are benign, just as the vast majority of real world interactions are benign. That said, there are at least a few unsavory people lurking in the digital shadows. Predators typically seek out kids who appear vulnerable to seduction, primarily teens who post sexually provocative photos or videos of themselves or others. So how often does stranger danger really occur? Studies show that about one in twenty-five kids has received an online sexual solicitation where the person at least suggested a real world meeting.[3] Usually exposure to sexual predators occurs through social media or chat forums designed for and/or heavily frequented by young people, including Facebook, Skout, Chatroulette, Omegle, Tumblr, Snapchat, and Instagram. And new venues for this behavior pop up constantly— every time kids decide some other site is the hot place to be.

That's a lot to worry about, and parents might think that the best way to protect their children is to keep them offline altogether. This does not work! Even if you take away your kids' laptops and smartphones, they can access the Internet at school, at the library, on their friends' devices, or on devices they purchase and use in secret. And do you really want to take your kids away from their number one social venue anyway?

How to Protect Your Kids

Following are some suggestions to help you protect your children from tech-driven addictions and other digital dangers:

- Limit privacy by insisting digital devices only be used in common areas of the home.
- Monitor your child's Internet use by checking computer bookmarks, history of websites accessed, and caches.
- Install filtering and monitoring software that prevents access to inappropriate content and provides parents with information about time spent online, websites visited, and people contacted. This software can be installed on computers, laptops, tablets, smartphones, and just about any other digital device.
- Set time limits on digital device usage tied to performance in school and doing chores.
- Consider using an Internet service provider that is "family oriented," blocking access to sexually inappropriate material. You

can ask your provider about parental controls. Be aware, however, that even the best of these providers can't catch everything.

- Advise your child never to reveal to anyone, without your permission, his or her full name, address, phone number, school, or any other information that would make your child easy to locate.
- Let your kids know that it is never acceptable to meet an online friend in person without your permission and supervision.
- Talk with your children about their Internet and smartphone activities. Encourage them to inform you of any online experiences or conversations that make them uncomfortable.
- Learn more about the digital devices your children use so you can better monitor their activities.
- Learn about the social media sites your children visit and post on so you can better monitor their activities.
- If you believe your child is being sexually exploited or that someone is attempting to exploit your child, report it to the police, the FBI, and the CyberTipline (www.cybertipline.com or 800-843-5678).

HELPING KIDS ALREADY INTO CYBERSEX

What happens if you discover that your son or daughter is already actively engaged in online sexual activity such as porn use, webcam sex, and sexting? At first it may not be clear if there is an actual problem or, if there is a problem, how serious it is. In other words, is this an occasional activity or is your child spending multiple hours online each day? Frankly, it can be difficult to discern the extent of a child's online activity because kids, especially teens, are often secretive about their behavior. Therefore, in addition to asking them directly about their computer activities, you may want to review what else is happening in their lives:

- Has their school performance dropped or are they maintaining their grades?
- Are they still engaging in their usual afterschool sports and social activities, or have they dropped out?

- Are they becoming moody, depressed, and anxious?
- Have they become more secretive about where and how they spend their time?
- Do they refuse to let you view their digital life?

Nearly always, the best path to understanding your teen's sex life is to talk to him or her about it in a nonjudgmental way. The biggest challenge many parents face when investigating this type of issue is to not overreact when experiencing fear or discomfort about a child's digital wanderings. Sometimes parents become overly angry, punitive, dismissive, or anxious after learning about a child's sexual activity. It is best if parents can work through their feelings about these issues before talking to their child, as fear-based and anger-based responses tend to drive away potentially valuable family growth moments. Again, the most important thing is talking to your child *in a nonjudgmental way*. There's a big difference between saying, "This morning I noticed some porn on your computer, and it makes me uncomfortable," and saying, "Oh my God, I cannot believe you are looking at that awful crap. You can forget about using the car this month *and* we're taking you to a therapist this very instant."

Note: It is essential that kids have helpful, well-researched, age-appropriate information about their own physical and sexual development. The better informed a child is, the less likely it is that seeing an inappropriate image or a parent's sexual activity is going to produce long-term harm. Most important, children need to feel that they can discuss sexual issues without shame, embarrassment, or judgment. Kids need to feel that they can talk to a parent or at least a professional counselor about anything.

We can't emphasize strongly enough how important it is for parents to work through their own reactions to pornography and whatever else their child may be looking at or doing sexually by discussing the issue with other parents or a therapist before talking to their child. Having done that, the parent should then try to learn the extent and purpose of the child's porn usage. If the behavior seems extreme or if it's being engaged in as an escape/avoidance mechanism, then it might be wise to seek the help of a supportive therapist. Parents should be careful in selecting a therapist, though, because there are very few professionals trained in the treatment of adolescent sexuality. Consider going to www.aasect.org, the website of the American Association of Sexuality Educators, Counselors, and Therapists. There you will find comprehensive referral information.

CHAPTER EIGHT

FROM DISCONNECTION TO INTIMACY: THE HEALING PROCESS

For years I put sex ahead of all else, even though I wasn't having much actual sex. Instead, I was looking at and masturbating to pornography, engaging in webcam mutual masturbation, and playing virtual reality sex games. A couple of times I started dating in real life, usually very nice women who were looking for a long-term relationship. One of them I really liked a lot. I loved the way she made me laugh. But I just wasn't ever really "there" with her. I was always thinking about going online later, after our date. Even on dates with her that ended in sex, I would rush home afterward and masturbate to porn. Eventually she broke up with me. She actually thought I was cheating on her from the way I behaved. And I was, in a way. Finally I just stopped dating altogether, since it never seemed to go anywhere. Then one day I woke up and I was thirty-five years old, I hadn't been on a date in several years, and I was really, really lonely and depressed. I talked about feeling depressed with a friend (the only one I had left), and he suggested seeing a psychiatrist. Thankfully, that doctor knew enough about sex addiction to figure out what was really going on with me. He referred me to a specialist, and that therapist worked with me and got me into Twelve Step recovery. As of today, I've been sober for six months and my depression has lifted. I'm not quite ready for dating, but I think I will be in time.

—Jerry, thirty-six, office manager

I am a wife and mother of three kids, and I'm also a sex and love addict. It sounds weird to call myself an addict, but there it is. I think I've always been this way a little bit, searching for a man who could "fix" me and make me feel okay about myself. But after I married Will, I kept it in check, deciding that even if the passion had worn off, I was married and that was that. Then my youngest started school and I had nothing to occupy my time. Will makes lots of money, so I didn't need to work and I never really enjoyed working anyway, so I stayed home and tried to stay busy. Unfortunately, that involved going online and flirting with men on social media and dating sites. I only had a few webcam flings to start, nothing in person, so I decided I wasn't really cheating. Then I discovered "friend finder" apps. That must be what drug addicts feel like when they discover crack cocaine. Unlike websites, apps geolocate guys for you, so suddenly I was chatting with guys right around the corner from me, and why "webcam" when we could hook up in person, you know? By the end of the first year, I'd been with probably a hundred guys, and the pace was increasing. If a day went by and I didn't have sex with a man other than Will, I got really irritable and nasty. I was ruining my marriage and I knew it, but I couldn't stop. Finally, Will found out what I was up to. He threatened to leave me unless I went to rehab. So I went to rehab, and now I'm in outpatient therapy and Twelve Step recovery. Staying sexually sober is really hard, and some days I want to just give up, but I haven't, and my life is slowly getting better.

—Moira, thirty-nine, wife and mother

Taking Steps Toward Healing

People who struggle with digital technology and compulsive sexual or romantic fantasies and behaviors need help to get better. Addicts cannot truly change their behavior by themselves. The very nature of addiction implies a kind of distorted thinking; therefore, the person with the problem needs both the insight and the accountability that only an objective outsider can provide. Declarations like, "I swear I will never look at online porn again," or, "As long as I live, I will never use another hookup app," or, "My webcam sex days are over," are not enough to keep a cybersex addict out of trouble when challenged by emotional or psychological discomfort. Without outside assistance, the temptation of emotional escape and dissociation through sexual/romantic arousal is simply too great. Any promises you've made to yourself and others that your cybersex days are over will fall by the wayside. However, changes can and do occur if you work toward them, with assistance, in a straightforward, honest, and open-minded fashion.

Here are the first action steps toward change:

1. **Find a professional therapist trained in the treatment of addictions AND sexual disorders.** A qualified certified sex addiction treatment specialist can help you to better understand the issues you present, educate you about what you have been and will be going through, what triggers it, and how to combat it. He or she can set you on a path toward long-term behavior change, accountability, and a life of sexual health. You will find more guidance toward finding the 'right' therapist for you in the next chapter, Getting Help, Getting Well.

2. **Find a support group.** Cybersex addicts, like other addicts, heal best when they are part of a recovering community. Most often, sex addicts who have the means will attend (in addition to therapy) Twelve Step sexual recovery groups like Sex Addicts Anonymous, Sexaholics Anonymous, Sexual Compulsives Anonymous, Sexual Recovery Anonymous, or Sex and Love Addicts Anonymous. There are also faith-based support groups and "smart recovery" groups for sexual addicts. Each support group is slightly different in tone and approach, so you may wish to check out several of them to see which program works best for you. You will also find guidance toward finding the 'right' support group for you in the next chapter, Getting Help, Getting Well.

3. **Find an accountability partner.** This is someone to help you be accountable for the work ahead—usually either a therapist specializing in sex and love addiction or a Twelve Step recovery program "sponsor." Your accountability partner's job is to assist you, either in person or by phone, with your commitments toward change—identifying what those commitments actually are and how you can best carry them out. Utilizing this person is an essential step toward healing. It is best to find a neutral person, ideally someone who is familiar with sex addiction and how to overcome it. Much of the time your accountability partner will be a person who has struggled with issues similar to your own. While it can initially feel embarrassing and silly to check in with another person about your behavior, keep in mind that if you really do have a problem, then you need help from others to get well.

4. **Throw out all physical material related to your problem.** If porn is your problem, throw out all books, magazines, DVDs, and flash drives that contain pornographic stories or imagery, along with any related paraphernalia such as sex toys or lubricants. Take everything to a commercial trash dumpster at least a mile from your home. Call your accountability partner to report that you've done this, and make a commitment to not purchase or otherwise acquire any new material related to your sexual or romantic acting out. Promise that if you are tempted to do so, you will call your accountability partner *before* acting on that temptation.

5. **Go through your computer files and smartphone *while being monitored by your accountability partner*.** Delete all downloaded files and emails with pictures or attachments related to your acting out. Use the computer's search capability to look for sexual or romantic items. For instance, if online porn is your issue, search for .gif, .tif, .jpeg, .wmv, .mpg, .mpeg, .mp4, .avi, and .mov files. Delete all contact information (emails, IM addresses,

webcam addresses, and phone numbers) for acting out partners. Delete all bookmarks on your browser related to your acting out. Eliminate any screen names you have used for sexual or romantic purposes. Delete written self-descriptions or personal photos used in conjunction with sexual acting out, including face shots and fully clothed pictures you have included in your online profile(s). On your phone, delete old sexts and texts from acting out partners. Delete any apps related to your acting out. For this entire process, ask your accountability partner to stay nearby to ensure that you are not longingly re-reading, looking at, or enjoying the material one last time before deleting it. There is no need to review the stuff; just get rid of it. If possible, disable the webcams on your digital devices.

6. **Cancel any memberships to websites, apps, and brick-and-mortar stores that service your problematic behavior.** You may want to also cancel the credit card you've used to pay for these so that your memberships don't automatically renew. If you don't want to cancel the card, call your credit card company and tell them you've lost it. They will happily send you a replacement with a new number, and this serves the same purpose.

7. **Stay away from "gray area" activities.** This is similar to recommending that an alcoholic not hang out in bars. There's an old recovery saying: If you go to the barbershop every day, eventually you'll get a haircut. So if you're a sex addict, don't go to R-rated, NC-17 rated, or unrated movies, don't leave the Victoria's Secret catalog sitting on the coffee table, and cancel your weekly massage (even if it's nonsexual). Leave these things to people who don't have your issue. They can handle them; you can't. When working toward change, you will have to find other, healthier hobbies and activities to both occupy your time and offer you healthy pleasures.

8. **Orient home or work computer in a public-facing direction so that other people can see what you're doing online.** When traveling, commit to using your laptop, smartphone, and other Internet-accessible devices only in public areas. At work, only go online during work hours, don't stay late to work on projects, and avoid being alone in the office. Wherever you are, commit to checking with your accountability partner both before and after you go online.

9. **Display inspirational photos**. Place pictures of your spouse/partner and kids around your work and home computer. Also use them as background imagery on your laptop, smartphone, and other portable devices. You might also use their voices or a song that reminds you of them as your ringtone. These reminders of what your problematic behavior might cost you can be a very powerful motivator.

10. **Purchase and install filtering/accountability software.** If you intend to use the Internet and your smartphone again—and for most people these things are "must haves" for both work and healthy socialization—then this suggestion is an absolute necessity. Although with enough effort any software can be defeated, at the very least filtering and accountability software provides time to reflect before acting out.

INTERNET FILTERING AND ACCOUNTABILITY SOFTWARE PROGRAMS

Happily, there are numerous "parental control" filtering and accountability software programs that sex and love addicts can use to protect themselves from their online behavior for phones, tablets, laptops and computers. As the parental control label suggests, most of these programs were initially developed to protect children from inappropriate content and contacts, but they can easily be adapted for use by recovering sex and love addicts.

When shopping for protective software, recovering sex addicts should consider the following:

1. **Customizable filtering and blocking.** Nearly all of these products have preset filtering levels—ranging from levels appropriate for young children to levels appropriate for adults who wish to stay away from certain types of sites/apps. The better ones offer customizable filtering, with blacklisting of specific sites/apps that would otherwise be allowed and whitelisting of specific sites/apps that would otherwise be blocked.

2. **Secondary filtering and blocking features.** In addition to website filtering and blocking, most products offer several secondary features, including the following:
    *   Online search filtering and blocking
    *   App blocking
    *   Social media blocking
    *   Instant message/chat blocking
    *   File transfer blocking (preventing the sending and/or receiving of pictures, videos, and the like)
    *   Video game filtering
    *   Profanity blocking

Obviously, some of these features are more important to recovering sex and love addicts than others. Software that includes all of these are best, though, as even video games may contain significant sexual content.

3. **Recording and reporting (accountability) features.** Ideally, protective softwares monitor the recovering sex addict's online activity and provide the addict's accountability partner with reports on usage, along with real time alerts if the addict uses or even attempts to use his or her digital device in a prohibited way. Available recording and reporting features may address the following:

    - Websites visited
    - Online searches
    - Social networking
    - Usernames and passwords
    - IM/chat
    - Email
    - Screenshot playback

    Ideally, reporting is available to accountability partners remotely (accessible via their own computer or phone) at regular intervals, on demand, and via real time alerts.

4. **Ease of use.** The software should be easy to install and to customize. Ideally, users should be able to globally configure the software, establishing settings on all of the sex addict's devices simultaneously instead of dealing with each machine individually. The best softwares offer free tech support via email, phone, text, and even live chat.

5. **Compatibility.** Not all softwares work on every digital device. In fact, many are quite limited and therefore not recommended for sex and love addicts, who usually have a wide array of devices on which to act out. It is important to make sure a product works on your particular device(s) before you purchase it. It is also important to see how many devices the license covers. Ideally, you want to cover all of your digital equipment with only one license.

Currently, the best filtering and accountability software products for use by recovering sex and love addicts are Net Nanny, Norton Family Premier, and WebWatcher. Annually updated reviews of filtering and accountability softwares can be found on the Sexual Recovery Institute's website at www.sexualrecovery.com/online-controls-for-sex-romance-addicts/.

Unfortunately, no protective software can guarantee sobriety. Even the best of these products is not infallible. In fact, a tech-savvy sex addict can eventually find ways to circumvent almost any protective program. As such, these products should not be thought of as enforcers of recovery. Instead, they should be viewed as tools of healing that can help an addict maintain sobriety and rebuild trust with a spouse or partner. At worst, a decent filtering and accountability software program may cause a sex or love addict to stop and think before circumventing the software and proceeding with a prohibited activity.

GOING COLD TURKEY

Some sex and love addicts need to take a brief break from digital technology. For these people, certain digital devices pose temptations that are too strong, inevitably leading them into acting out, and they must stay away until they have established a foundation in healing. People who need to temporarily abstain from the Internet and smartphone apps can purchase an old-fashioned (non-Internet enabled) cellphone, permitting them to stay in touch with friends and family without the ability to look at porn. Most of these phones still allow you to text, but not to send or receive attachments with those texts, so you can stay safe while still keeping in contact with your text-crazy kids.

Needless to say, removing oneself from digital interactivity altogether, even for a short period, can be a very frustrating experience for anyone used to connecting at the touch of a button. Many addicts become angry or defensive when a period of digital abstinence is suggested. Sometimes they try going online again to prove their ability to do so without acting out, only to find themselves in trouble once more.

> *Although I really did feel committed to staying out of my sexual problem areas, it was so easy to pop onto a porn site "just to see if there were any new videos." I seemed to have endless legitimate reasons to be online and, once there, the porn sites were just a click away. I couldn't seem to stay out of them. For a while I actually had to downgrade my phone and take my computer out of the house and give it to my accountability partner. This was the only way I could guarantee that I would not act out. It was really difficult, and I felt like a child deprived of his favorite toys, but it really helped with my recovery.*
> —Richard, twenty-five, DJ

Defining and Committing to Long-Term Change (Cybersex Sobriety)

Whereas simply reading this book is a good step toward change, keeping your forward momentum involves rolling up your sleeves and getting to work. The basis of that work starts with a plan for healing. This means you must create a bottom line definition of the behaviors you are going to stop. One term for not engaging in these behaviors, once they are defined, is "sexual sobriety."

People entering sex addiction treatment or Twelve Step sexual recovery programs typically have little to no idea what sexual sobriety really means or entails. This confusion is in sharp contrast to nearly any alcoholic or drug addict entering recovery, who more or less knows that being sober requires total abstinence from alcohol and/or illicit drugs. Not surprisingly, the most frequently asked question by newcomers to sex addiction recovery is: "Am I ever going to be able to have a healthy, regular sex life, or will I have to give up sex forever?" This question is usually followed by a statement like, "If I have to give up sex permanently, then you can forget my staying in treatment."

Fortunately, unlike sobriety for alcoholism and drug addiction, sexual sobriety is not defined by ongoing abstinence. Rather than total abstinence, sex and love addicts delineate, working in conjunction with a sex addiction treatment specialist and/or their Twelve Step sponsor, the specific sexual and romantic behaviors that are causing them significant problems. They then agree in a written sexual sobriety contract to completely abstain from those activities while, at the same time, engaging in non-problematic sexual and romantic behaviors only moderately and appropriately. In this way, sex and love addiction treatment addresses sobriety in much the same way it is handled with eating disorders—another area where sobriety does not mean permanently abstaining.

TIME OUT

Though abstinence is not a long-term goal, sometimes, especially early in the healing process, a short period of sexual abstinence—in essence a "time out" from all sexual behaviors, including masturbation—is both helpful and recommended. This period of complete sexual abstinence is suggested because most sex addicts new to recovery experience difficulty when trying to distinguish between healthy and unhealthy sexual behaviors. This brief period of being nonsexual can also help the addict develop some basic coping skills that can be used to both recognize and combat the emotional triggers and external circumstances that cue the addiction. Furthermore, as sex addicts struggle to avoid their "automatic" sexual choices, they gain much needed insight into the full extent of their past dependency on sex for emotional distraction and self-stabilization.

ABOUT MASTURBATION

One potentially problematic gray area for many recovering sex addicts is masturbation. For porn addicts and compulsive masturbators, the decision is clear—masturbation with or without pornography is not acceptable. For other addicts the solution may be less obvious. For some, masturbation can be an integral part of the addictive cycle—directly feeding the fantasies that produce the "high" of sexual or romantic addiction, thereby serving as a gateway to bottom line acting out behaviors. For these people, masturbation could be either a risky but still-sober behavior or a bottom line non-sober behavior. For other sex addicts, non-compulsive masturbation can actually aid the healing process, encouraging appropriate intimacy and contributing to an overall sense of sexual health and wellbeing.

In the same way that drug detoxification is the first step toward healing from substance abuse, a period of complete sexual abstinence—a detox from abusing sex—can be a first step on the road to long-term sexual sobriety. Again, sexual abstinence is *not* a long-term goal. Rather, it helps interrupt long-established compulsive behavior patterns while ego strength, social skills, and new coping mechanisms are developed. Essentially, sex addiction clinicians encourage this short period of complete sexual abstinence—usually thirty, sixty, or ninety days—not to deny addicts' dependency and intimacy needs, but to make them aware that there are other and better ways to get those needs met. In fact, the heavy lifting of sex addiction recovery is not this short time out from romantic and sexual behavior; rather, it is the slow (re)introduction of healthy sexuality.

THE SEXUAL BOUNDARY PLAN

If sexual sobriety doesn't require total sexual abstinence, what does it involve? Generally speaking, to achieve sobriety a sex addict must define the behaviors that do not compromise or destroy his or her values, life circumstances, and relationships. This is best done working in conjunction with a knowledgeable sex addiction therapist, a Twelve Step recovery sponsor, or some other accountability partner. The addict then commits in a *written sexual sobriety contract* to engage only in sexual behavior that is permitted within the bounds of that predetermined pact. As long as the addict's behavior remains within his or her concretely defined boundaries, the individual is sexually sober. It is important that these plans be put in writing and that they clearly define the addict's bottom line behaviors to be eliminated.

> *In my head I knew what I needed to change and how I needed to change it. But somehow I always ended up fooling myself and getting back into trouble. In the moment, I would somehow justify why something was okay for me to do, even though I had previously said that it wasn't okay. It wasn't until I wrote down what I needed to change, and committed to this with another person present, that I found the accountability and clarity to remain sober from my cybersex behaviors.*
> —Manny, forty-three, factory worker

The foundation of sex addiction recovery planning is a set of goals unique to the addict. When writing out your detailed sexual sobriety plan, you will first list all the reasons you want to make changes in your behavior. Then, having stated your personal goals, you will create a boundary plan that addresses your particular addictive fantasies and behaviors. Go to page 197 in the Activity Resources to complete your sexual boundary plan.

Writing a sexual boundary plan is not easy. Some will cringe at the idea of placing written limitations on their sex or love life. Some will say that a boundary plan might get in the way of spontaneity or intimacy. Some of these steps may even seem contrived or trivial. Keep in mind that learning to tolerate your discomfort with change is a major part of growth. Living in health, without shame, is the goal, and new ideas—even the uncomfortable ones—may serve you better than the practices you formerly relied on. The most important thing you can do to heal may be the one thing that didn't occur to you, so taking on potentially uncomfortable suggestions will likely pay off in the long run.

About Withdrawal

When quitting substances taken regularly for some time, many drug addicts face a variety of withdrawal symptoms, both physical and emotional. Likewise, those abusing sexual and romantic fantasies and behaviors also tend to experience withdrawal (mostly emotional) when they stop or alter their long-practiced behavior patterns. This experience varies from person to person, of course. If you recognize withdrawal symptoms in yourself, talk about them with others—a therapist, a Twelve Step sponsor or program member, or friends and family who understand what you are going through. Your discomfort is normal, but if experienced in the extreme, it should be brought to a professional therapist as soon as possible.

Some of the more common withdrawal symptoms include:

- **Longing and craving for connection:** For most cybersex addicts, their sexual acting out history has long masked underlying psychological conditions such as depression, anxiety, low self-esteem, and unresolved trauma. Without constant sex or romantic intrigue as a distraction, these conditions may now manifest as unbearable loneliness, neediness, anger, fear, or unhappiness. You may long for some relationship you fear you will never have, or feel as if there is something missing that you can never find or locate. These feelings are normal and to be expected. You are grieving the loss of an adaptive coping mechanism. However, if you find yourself avoiding daily responsibilities such as work or other commitments, neglecting basic self-care, or actually having fantasies or plans of suicide, it is essential to get professional help right away.
- **Irritability:** It is typical for withdrawal to evoke a great deal of irritability and anger over issues that to others are normal, ordinary annoyances. Just as some emotions previously masked by sexual obsessions manifest as depression, others may now be expressed as anger or frustration. If you can tolerate these feelings without screaming at your boss or kicking the cat, there is much to be learned. It is common for people who sexually act out to avoid

certain types of confrontation and to bury their angry feelings by dissociating through the acting out behavior. Learning what provokes your anger and how to manage it is a first step toward better self-care and better relationships. People in withdrawal are not always fun to be around, but it is essential for them to experience, tolerate, and survive these early difficult emotions.

- **Honeymooning:** In the first stages of change, you may lose all desire to sexually act out. It's as if you have been cured! You may be intrigued by the insight you are gaining, excited to have finally found a possible solution to your long-term problems, or still shocked from whatever crisis it was that caused you to examine your behavior in the first place. While this break can be a gift and an opportunity to gain knowledge, support, and direction, it can also be confusing, because the desire to act out will certainly return—likely stronger than ever. If this is not anticipated, it is easy to think that something went wrong, when actually the return of these feelings is a very normal part of the process. Healing doesn't mean the urge to sexually act out will completely go away. It does mean that these feelings can lessen over time as you learn how not to act on them.

- **Switching:** It is not unusual for those with histories of sexual acting out to switch their compulsive behavior from sex to other forms of problematic behavior, that is, to develop cross-addictions or co-occurring addictions. For example, it is common for the man who stops masturbating to porn to begin eating compulsively and quickly gain weight. Others may return to addictions long ago left behind, such as smoking cigarettes or using marijuana.

THE GIFTS OF HEALING

Recovering from the effects of compulsive cybersexuality can foster a rediscovery of self. Time formerly spent on obsessive online cruising, flirtation, sexting, porn, webcam sex, and the like may now go into family involvement, creativity, healthy recreation, and work. Time previously lost to searching for the hottest videos or cybersex partners can now go into hobbies, self-care, and connecting with loved ones.

If you are married or in a committed relationship, your healing will bring you a deeper understanding of both your own and your partner's emotional needs and wants, while encouraging you to become more vulnerable and intimate within your relationship. If you are not in a committed relationship, you can begin to build true self-esteem by making healthy choices regarding commitment, dating, and romantic partnering, and developing clearer definitions of healthy sexuality.

In the healing process, honesty, integrity, self-knowledge, and a deep desire to be known will slowly replace secrets, isolation, and superficiality. The healing process, when taken on actively and with motivation, offers a deepening level of maturity and hope for truly loving relationships. Efforts made toward change now will pay big dividends over time—if you are willing to do the work fully and honestly.

CHAPTER NINE

GETTING HELP,
GETTING WELL

*When I first started going to the Men's Commitment in Marriage sup-
port group at my church, I struggled to find the courage to just get a
few phone numbers from the other guys. Then, actually getting myself
to call people and ask for help when I needed it felt like an impossible
task. Finally, finding one person—an accountability partner—who
really got to know all about me and my problem, made a huge difference. It gave me someone who was further along in the healing process
than I was to ask for direction and guidance. With him on my side, I
started to feel like someone was there for me 24/7. So when that urge
to act out came in the middle of the night or during some lonely weekend, I could always call him and he was there to help. More than once,
making that simple phone call has kept me sexually sober.*

—Larry, forty-four, lab tech

*When I first entered therapy for my sex and love addiction, my thera-
pist suggested that I attend some sex addiction Twelve Step meetings to
get some external support. In the beginning, I went to SAA meetings
because there were lots of them in my city to choose from. But most
of the time I was the only woman in the room, and I felt uncomfortable sharing and being honest. Finally I told my therapist that I
felt restricted in those meetings. She smiled and suggested that I try a
different program, SLAA, telling me I'd find a lot more women there*

than in SAA. And she was right. I don't know how it is in other places,
but where I live SLAA is definitely the most welcoming program for
females. Now I have my therapist, plus a sponsor and a great group of
supportive women who are dealing with issues similar to mine. We call
each other all the time, and whenever one of us is struggling, the rest of
us rally around her. Maintaining my sobriety is much easier now that
I'm not trying to do it all on my own.

—Rhea, 27, sales representative

Anyone who has spent time recovering from an addiction knows that the first steps toward healing involve acknowledging the need for help, asking for help, and accepting that help. So whether you are an isolated porn abuser or an extrovert who carries out multiple app-enabled extramarital affairs simultaneously, the road to change is best not taken alone. Though many components of cybersex and porn addiction recovery involve solitude and self-reflection, nothing replaces the insight and accountability that interaction with other people provides, especially if those people are knowledgeable about sex and love addiction.

As noted in chapter eight, spouses are typically not the best people to turn to as a primary source of initial support in your recovery. The challenges just hit too close to home for them. As such, they are rarely able to be objective about your new commitments, and therefore they are not good sources of unbiased, nonjudgmental support. Yes, you probably want forgiveness from your partner, but it's better to seek help from another recovery resource first, as actions speak louder than words. That said, spouses do have a right to know about your sobriety plans and your ongoing efforts toward recovery. If they ask to be informed, you should honor that request, but sometimes it is best to do so with a professional present.

Even longtime good friends aren't the best people to turn to for the help and direction you need in your process of healing. After all, some of those friends may have been enabling your behavior in the first place.

Even after I lost a job I really liked because I was using my work laptop
and smartphone for sex, it was hard to get my friends to take the issue

seriously. Looking back now, I can see that I needed someone to chal-
lenge me on my thinking and help me stop my acting out behaviors,
but all that my friends ever did was congratulate me on being such a
"player."

—Ross, twenty-seven, investment broker

Usually, the people who are best able to provide support and useful guidance are those with similar problems who are also in the process of healing. These people can be found in therapy groups, in Twelve Step recovery programs for sex and love addicts, and in faith-based support groups focused on sex and love addiction. One-on-one therapy with a sex addiction treatment specialist can also be extremely helpful, especially in the early stages of the healing process when you are working to understand your issues and to develop a sexual sobriety plan. Ultimately, though, recovering sex and love addicts need the support and self-reflective mirror provided by other recovering addicts. Plus, having a handy list of supportive people in recovery is essential when you feel the impulse to act out, need immediate help, or simply want to vent your frustrations.

Healthy places to find help with your recovery include:

- Individual psychotherapy focused on sex addiction
- Therapy groups focused on sex addiction
- Twelve Step recovery groups for sex addicts
- Faith-based support groups focused on sex addiction
- An accountability partner who is familiar with sex addiction recovery (ideally another recovering person)
- Inpatient treatment and/or intensive outpatient treatment programs for sex addicts
- Ongoing relationships with supportive people who know all about your sexual behavior and are willing to be called anytime you need help

At a minimum, your commitment to recovery must entail the following:

- Engaging other people who have traveled down the road you're on
- Developing a written sexual boundary plan
- Having a person or people to whom you're accountable

GETTING INTO THERAPY

Getting therapy with a sex addiction treatment specialist is one of the most helpful steps you can take at any point in the healing process. The therapy setting provides a safe place to discuss the feelings you are having and the challenges you are facing. Additionally, a qualified therapist can serve as both an accountability partner and an objective guide toward self-awareness, helping you to develop, over time, an understanding of why and how you came to engage in your addictive sexual or romantic behaviors.

Unfortunately, finding the right therapist is not always easy. In the past, incorrect psychiatric diagnoses were often used to categorize sexually impulsive and addictive behavior. Sadly, this still occurs in the present. It is actually relatively easy for some therapists not trained to deal with sex addiction to misidentify the issue as a mood disorder such as severe anxiety or depression. This typically happens when the clinician does not recognize that these concurrent disorders are related to compulsive sexual or romantic behaviors and perhaps to the stress of trying to hide those behaviors.

In reality, mood disorders are far more common than sex and love addiction, and therapists are well-trained in their identification and diagnosis. Thus, these accompanying symptoms are often mistaken as an addict's primary issue. Even when a clinician recognizes the severity of a patient's out-of-control sexual behavior, the patient can easily be misdiagnosed as having bipolar, obsessive compulsive, generalized anxiety, or dissociative identity disorder—all of which can present with an element of compulsive sexual behavior—even though these psychiatric disorders are not an underlying condition for most sex and love addicts. In fact, mood problems typically clear up on their own after a sex addict achieves and maintains a modicum of sexual or romantic sobriety.

Furthermore, our current lack of a clear, clinical, criteria-based psychiatric diagnosis for hypersexual behavior has left the door open for some mental health and addiction professionals to use the label "sex addict" to promote treatment agendas that are more focused on moral, cultural, or religious values than purely clinical values. These misguided clinicians often do more harm than good, labeling people seeking insight or help with non-pathological issues like fetish behaviors or same-sex arousal as sexually addicted. Sadly, the tendency of certain moralistic clinicians to engage in agenda-based treatment gives the real sex and love addiction treatment field a bad name and makes an already confusing issue that much harder to understand and diagnose.

Another common problem encountered by people seeking help for addictive sexual behavior is crossing paths with well-intentioned "sex positive" therapists who are more invested in enabling addicts' behaviors than in stopping them. It is not helpful to a sex or love addict for a counselor to offer advice like, "Maybe you're being too hard on yourself," or, "You should just loosen up and allow yourself to become more comfortable with that," or, "That's just what adults do," when the activities the addict just described are compulsive and consistently creating distress and negative consequences. While this may be an effective therapeutic approach for people with other kinds of sexual problems, such as being uncomfortable with fetish or same-sex behaviors, this well-intended advice is exactly the wrong approach for people whose lives have become increasingly interrupted, diminished, and harmed by compulsive sexual and romantic behavior patterns.

The therapist I went to didn't see a problem with my sexual behavior.
He just saw me as a single man with a healthy sexual appetite. Despite
my complaints about the lost time, lost energy, lost focus, and lost job
(because I kept misusing my work-issued laptop and iPhone), he kept
insisting that I shouldn't be so hard on myself, that I was struggling

with "integrating my sexuality," and that when I was more self-accepting I would feel better about my fantasies and behaviors. Finally, after several months of this and my behavior and depression only getting worse, I went to see someone else. Luckily, this second therapist understood sexual addiction, and I've started on the path to getting better.

—Carl, thirty-three, pharmacist

If you find yourself in a similar situation to Carl in the example above, discuss your thoughts and feelings with your therapist, and, if he or she is unwilling or unable to help you properly, look for someone who can, mostly likely a therapist trained in sex addiction treatment. (See Resources on page 185.)

Locating Qualified Therapists

Because there are many different types of helping professionals, choosing the right one can be confusing. The basic choices include psychiatrist, psychologist, master's level counselor (which includes secular and pastoral counselor), licensed social worker, addiction counselor, and marriage and family therapist. When choosing a clinician, more important than the person's specific academic degree and job title is that the counselor you are considering has some knowledge of and training in sex addiction, or at least an understanding of addictive disorders in general.

Keep in mind that the person you choose as your therapist should never be a friend, neighbor, or family member. Despite their potential good intentions and offers of free or low-cost help, it is highly problematic and unethical for psychotherapists to enter into a professional relationship with someone they already know. It is also not a good idea to barter or trade goods or other services for psychotherapy. It is best to see someone you do not yet know, and to use cash, insurance, or a combination of both to pay for your treatment.

Often, a good way to find a qualified sex addiction treatment specialist is to ask around at support group meetings for a referral. Nearly always, by listening to and spending time with other sex and love addicts in recovery, you can get a sense of what is working for them. If asked, most will be happy to tell you about their experiences with therapy—past and present, good and bad—and to offer recommendations.

Another excellent source for referrals is the Society for the Advancement of Sexual Health (www.sash.net). SASH maintains a list of professionals knowledgeable about sex addiction, organized by state. In particular, look for clinicians with sex and love addiction treatment credentials, most notably the "CSAT" designation. You can locate them by geographic area through the sexhelp.com website. Many of the nationally known drug and alcohol treatment centers also maintain lists of therapists who are trained in sexual disorders and sex addiction treatment. These treatment facilities can provide names of knowledgeable therapists in your community, as can the community centers found in most urban areas of the United States and Canada.

Many larger corporations and most unions offer workers access to an employee assistance program. EAP counselors often have addiction training, though only rarely are they knowledgeable about sex addiction. If you have health insurance, check your insurance plan to see what diagnoses are covered and which therapists you can use. Unfortunately, most insurance plans do not cover treatment for sexual issues. Nevertheless, many people dealing with sex and love addiction also struggle with depression, anxiety, and other psychological problems that are covered by insurance, and sex addicts often request and receive coverage for those issues, getting treatment for their addiction at the same time.

EVALUATING A POTENTIAL THERAPIST

Before launching yourself into a long-term therapeutic arrangement, it is wise to make sure that a particular clinician is the right therapist for you. Pay attention to how meeting with him or her makes you feel. Do you feel understood? Do you feel that this person has the knowledge to help you? Do you feel that the therapist is being genuine when meeting with you? Is the therapist taking the time to really listen to you, or does he or she seem more interested in hearing himself or herself talk? Most important: Did you get the sense that the therapist would be willing to confront you about behaviors and activities that you know are unhealthy, or do you worry that the therapist might allow you to distract them or to make serious mistakes without challenging you?

Addiction treatment differs significantly from traditional therapy, and you should be sure a prospective therapist hears your particular concerns and can help you grow in your recovery. To determine whether a therapist is able to handle your issues, you can evaluate his or her experience and attitudes by asking addiction-specific questions. You should also feel comfortable discussing the length of time your treatment may take, the frequency of your sessions, and fees the therapist expects to receive. Remember that an exploratory meeting does not in any way commit you to ongoing therapy with that particular therapist. You may wish to "interview" several clinicians before deciding which person will best meet your needs.

Here are some sample questions to ask a prospective therapist:

- Do you understand sex and love addiction?
- Have you ever treated a sex or love addict?
- What is your experience with sex addiction, with compulsive behaviors in general, with other addictions?
- Do you recommend that your addicted clients attend Twelve Step meetings?
- How familiar are you with geolocating sex apps, online porn abuse and related technologies?
- Are you familiar with the concepts taught in Alcoholics Anonymous and related programs?
- Are you comfortable and familiar with treating sexual issues?
- How would you support my sexual and romantic sobriety?
- How would you help me if I acted out in my addiction?
- If applicable: Are you experienced with lesbian, gay, bisexual, or transgender clients?
- If applicable: How will you address or handle my religious beliefs?

THERAPEUTIC CHOICES

While many therapists prefer to work one-on-one in individual therapy with clients, the preferred method of treatment for most addictive behaviors is group therapy. Generally a treatment specialist works with a group of between six and ten addicts. A facilitated group setting allows patients to see that their problem is not unique, which helps in reducing the shame associated with sexual acting out. The group format is also ideal for confronting the denial and rationalizations common among sex addicts. Such confrontations are powerful not just for the addict being confronted, but for the addicts doing the confronting, helping everyone present learn how denial, minimization, justification, and rationalization sustain addictive behaviors. Addicts are also able to learn what works and what doesn't based on other members' experience, strength, and hope.

If a sex addiction therapy group is not available in your area, many aspects of sex addiction support groups can be used to supplement individual therapy. In fact, seeing an outpatient therapist while actively participating in one or more sexual recovery support groups works quite well for most people.

Addicts experiencing a severe emotional or life crisis related to their sexual or romantic acting out or who are unable to stop acting out despite professional help and active participation in a support group may require an intensive outpatient or even an inpatient treatment program. These more rigorous treatment settings offer a higher level of care than you can get from standard outpatient therapy and support groups, with programs designed for addicts who are struggling with profound depression, anxiety, and severe life crises in addition to their addiction.

In nearly all cases, the best first step in getting help is to meet one-on-one with a well-trained sex addiction treatment professional. He or she can then guide you in your personal process of healing.

COUPLES THERAPY

Couples who are dealing with a recent discovery that one partner is a sex or love addict, or that there has been extensive infidelity and betrayal by one partner in the relationship, need a special kind of support. Least helpful is the clinician who is reactive and brings into the therapy room a preconceived notion that betrayed spouses should just leave or kick the cheater out. These therapists simply don't understand that partners dealing with betrayal—even on a massive scale—often do not want to lose the relationship over it. They are most often in shock. When seeking a couples counselor, it is critical to select one who is willing to help you work toward your goals—as individuals and as a couple—whatever those goals might be. Find someone who can hear your story objectively and nonjudgmentally, without a hidden agenda.

Sometimes the addict, so eager to seek forgiveness in the beginning, needs the therapist's help to contain his or her anxiety and fear of abandonment. Otherwise, a hurt and angry betrayed partner ends up having to soothe and reassure the addict, which is not healthy for either person. At the same time, an astute therapist can help the betrayed partner communicate his or her feelings of hurt, loss, and anger. In these and many other ways the right professional can help a couple negotiate the early stages of healing, directing the addict toward the required structure and help, and encouraging spouses to educate themselves about the issues and providing support for the hurt and anger they are feeling. The therapist can also guide the process of disclosure, helping to reduce the power of long-held sexual secrets.

> In the beginning, couples therapy allowed me access to truths about our relationship that had been covered up for so long. As much as I hated hearing it, I needed to know everything that my husband had lied about, and the disclosure process was essential. It helped me stop blaming myself so much, and it allowed me to see the kind of problem he had even before he met me. Later in the therapy, when I wasn't so angry, I began to examine how closed off I had become to him and to myself, how I had slowly accepted living with someone who wasn't emotionally there, and what that cost me. I think it really helped for my husband to be present in the counseling sessions and to hear my side of the story. This helped both of us learn what to do differently if we were going to move forward together.
>
> —Alice, fifty-seven, wife of a recovering sex addict

A couples therapist sees the couple together. Sometimes, that therapist also meets with each member of the couple individually or, more rarely and usually less successfully, sees only one member of the couple for individual therapy. No matter what, when you're dealing with concerns this sensitive, it's best to seek out a therapist who's thoroughly versed in treating sex and love addiction and who has experience providing help to couples dealing with this disorder. It is also best to work with a professional who has a "no secrets" policy. A couples therapist who holds sexual or related secrets from one partner while working with both members of the couple is destined to fail. Though it may be effective to hold on to some information until it is ready to be healthfully disclosed, a good therapist will not promise to keep any secrets long-term.

Twelve Step Support Groups

Twelve Step support groups are among the most useful, readily available, affordable, and easily utilized tools for healing from addiction. These programs have helped millions to recover, one day at a time, from addictions as varied as alcoholism, drug addiction, compulsive gambling, compulsive spending, eating disorders, and sex and love addiction. Twelve Step meetings—all of which are based on the time-tested teachings of Alcoholics Anonymous—offer peer support, shame reduction, and guidance, along with an ongoing model for hope and change.

Numerous Twelve Step programs for sex and love addiction are available. Sexaholics Anonymous (SA), Sex Addicts Anonymous (SAA), Sexual Compulsives Anonymous (SCA), Sex and Love Addicts Anonymous (SLAA), and Sexual Recovery Anonymous (SRA) are all nationwide programs for sex addicts. SLAA is the best program for love addicts. Some meetings are open to anyone who wishes to attend, while others (identified as "closed meetings") are open only to those who identify as sexually or romantically addicted. A few meetings are gender-specific or LGBT-specific. Before attending, it is best to check by calling the group's local hotline number, which can easily be found online or in the phone book.

While not all the answers to healing sexually and romantically addictive behaviors are found in Twelve Step meetings, the principles espoused by Twelve Step programs and the fellowship and support they lend to the recovery process are invaluable to addicts committed to healing. At meetings, ask for phone numbers of people who are willing to support your healing process. Get involved in this community of people by making friends with and being of service to others in the program.

TWELVE STEP SUPPORT GROUP Q AND A

Despite the usefulness of Twelve Step programs, some cybersex addicts object to attending or participating. Whether out of shame, fear of discovery, or the misperception that Twelve Step groups are some kind of cult, many would rather "go it alone" than attend a Twelve Step meeting. Unfortunately, going it alone is exactly what got them in trouble in the first place. For many addicts, just getting to their first meeting is the hardest part. This usually stems from anxiety and lack of accurate information. To address this, a Twelve Step support group Q and A is provided below.

Q: I am concerned about being seen at these meetings and people talking about me because I have been there. How private is a Twelve Step meeting?

A: Ironically, it is often the same men and women who post nude pictures of themselves on dating sites and smartphone hookup apps—risking relationships and public humiliation—who balk at the idea of walking into a Twelve Step meeting. While it is true that the meetings are not bound to the same level of confidentiality as a therapy group, all participants of Twelve Step programs are committed to anonymity as a part of their own healing process. Many sex addiction recovery meetings are "closed," meaning they are available only to sex and love addicts, which adds an extra layer of safety. In almost every case, the benefits of attending a meeting far outweigh the possible negative consequences. And remember, people who see you there don't want to be talked about outside the meeting any more than you do.

Q: I don't want to have to talk about myself publicly. Will they make me do this?

A: Other than introducing yourself by your first name only, participation in Twelve Step meetings is entirely voluntary. No one will make you talk about anything that you don't wish to divulge.

Q: I have heard that a lot of freaks and sex offenders go to these meetings. Is that true? My problems haven't really hurt anybody other than myself, and I don't think I will feel comfortable around a bunch of sex offenders.

A: A wide range of people attend sex and love addiction recovery meetings, from those who are court-mandated to those whose behaviors harm no one but themselves. Believe it or not, there is something to be gained from hearing almost everyone's story at the meetings. At the end of each meeting, you can decide whom you would like to get to know better and whose example you want to follow.

Q: I have heard that there is a lot of emphasis in these meetings on religion. I don't feel comfortable with all that God stuff and I certainly don't want to trade my sexual problems for being involved in a cult. What is the deal with this?

A: Twelve Step groups are definitely not cults. They do, however, use phrases like "higher power" and "a power greater than ourselves" to help addicts put their faith in something beyond their own best thinking. The word "God" is used as well, usually followed by the words "as we understand God," creating a lot of leeway for those who struggle with organized religion and the "God of their childhood." The reference to "God" in the Twelve Steps is not in any way directed toward a specific religion or belief system.

Q: I hear that more people get picked up for sex in those meetings than actually get well. Is that true?

A: If your goal is finding sex, you probably know by now that you can pretty much find it anywhere. If you go to a Twelve Step meeting looking for the support of people who have long periods of sexual healing—people who can and will lend you a helping hand—then that is what you will find. If you go to a Twelve Step meeting in hookup mode, you may be able to persuade someone to be sexual with you. In general, however, the meetings are safe, supportive places. That said, it is always best to get together with new members only in public, staying at the meeting places or perhaps a coffee shop. It is also best to avoid getting too involved with one member too quickly, as intense relationships are often a hallmark of sexual and romantic addiction.

Q: What is a sponsor and how do I choose one?

A: Sponsors are personal guides to healing and staying sober, usually not friends to begin with and *never* lovers. Typically, a sponsor is someone of the same gender who has been in recovery long enough to have achieved some success. He or she should be active in the recovery meetings and have worked through the Twelve Steps. In addition, a sponsor's personal situation should somewhat match your own so that he or she can help guide you more individually. For example, if you are married with kids, a sponsor who is also married with kids might be preferable. If you are HIV-positive, it might be helpful to have an HIV-positive sponsor. You choose a sponsor by listening to various people at meetings until you hear someone who resonates with you. When you find someone you connect with, you simply approach that person before or after a meeting and ask, "Are you available to be a sponsor and, if so, would you like to have coffee and hear my story?" This is the best way to start. If that person says "no," don't take it personally or give up; just ask someone else.

FAITH-BASED SUPPORT GROUPS

Twelve Step groups are spiritual programs, but not religious. For people to whom a specific religion is important, there are multiple faith-based resources and strategies for healing. These can be used in conjunction with or separate from individual therapy, group therapy, and Twelve Step programs. Twelve Step programs are compatible with any religion. Happily, there are many well-constructed and well-run faith-based recovery groups for cybersex and porn addicts. The best of these programs focus on shame reduction, peer support, accountability, and hope.

We do not recommend faith-based programs that attempt to alter an addict's behavior by shaming the person or by insisting that prayer or spiritual study or even being of service, in and of themselves, will "fix" the problem and eliminate the acting out. Fortunately, many faith-based programs today are non-shaming, accountability based, and highly supportive—recognizing that sex addicts are not "morally challenged people" who lack the willpower needed to control their sexual and romantic behaviors, but people dealing with serious emotional and psychological pain who need empathetic support and direction.

FINDING HELP OUTSIDE URBAN AREAS

Life in the big city offers many opportunities both for sexual acting out and for healing. In most large urban areas there are numerous therapists to choose from, along with an array of Twelve Step and other self-help meetings. Although people living outside urban areas typically have the same basic opportunities for acting out as their urban counterparts—digital technology goes everywhere, after all—they may have significantly fewer resources for healing. This doesn't, however, mean that help is unavailable to those living in less populated areas. In fact, the same digital technologies that make acting out so easy, no matter your location, can also assist in recovery.

The following are some useful suggestions for people living in suburban or rural environments:

- **Join an online support group.** Most Twelve Step sexual recovery programs have online meetings in addition to in-person meetings. They offer long-distance peer support and sponsorship by phone, email, or webcam. Many recovering people participate in regular weekly chats online, gaining strength and support from people all over the world. Many Twelve Step programs also publish newsletters and have other reading materials that are available online.

- **Attend a recovery event.** Many Twelve Step programs hold annual conventions and conferences in different parts of the United States and around the world. These are great opportunities to connect with others who are recovering from sex and love addiction.

- **Attend counseling remotely.** Some therapists are willing to counsel clients over the telephone, via email, or using webcams. These professionals are usually easy to find online.

- **Read self-help and recovery literature.** A great deal of reading material devoted to sex addiction is available through online bookstores and libraries. Most of this material can be downloaded to an e-reader or smartphone. Additionally, Twelve Step sex and love addiction recovery groups make a great deal of their program materials available online for free.

- **Download recovery apps.** There are many smartphone apps designed to assist people who are healing from addiction. A few of these apps are focused on cybersex addiction, though most are general recovery-related apps that provide encouraging messages throughout the day, meditative thoughts, or access to helpful literature. Some of the most useful apps are "meeting finder" apps. So in the same way you can geolocate potential sex partners, you can geolocate the next nearby Twelve Step meeting.

- **Purchase and install filtering/accountability software.** These programs, discussed in detail in chapter eight, are designed to prevent you from accessing problematic websites and apps, and to inform your accountability partner if you are misusing a digital device. These softwares are relatively inexpensive and highly adaptable for use by sex and love addicts in recovery, so there is no reason to not use them.

Keys to Maintaining Change

As any person healing from a compulsive or addictive behavior will tell you, the keys to real behavior change are quite simple:

- Acceptance of your problem
- Motivation to change
- Willingness to be honest with others and to let them help you
- Finding and maintaining accountability

Those who are truly committed to changing their sexual behaviors will go along with sometimes annoying and unfamiliar rituals and situations, experiment with uncomfortable, difficult feelings, and report to people they barely know—all because they don't want to continue their addiction. If you have had negative external consequences, such as relationship, health, legal, financial, or other crises, that have motivated you to commit to no longer defining your life by sexual and/or romantic fantasies and behaviors, then you are among those most likely to stay with the process and to experience long-term change.

Conversely, if you are seeking help simply to calm an upset partner, to accommodate a court order or an angry boss, or to superficially feel better about yourself—while continuing to act out in some hidden way—you will probably discover that it becomes harder and harder to live a double life while gaining self-knowledge and awareness. At some point you will either have to commit fully to recovery, or you will end up re-engaging with the ever-deepening downward spiral of compulsive acting out. Those who choose the latter path continue to experience negative consequences as a result of their behavior. If they are lucky, they eventually return to the healing process with a true commitment to change.

SLIPS VS. RELAPSE

As with all addictions, sexual addiction "slips" and "relapse" are common and are to be expected in the early stages of healing.

It is important to distinguish a slip from a relapse. A slip is a brief, mostly unintended return to acting out. Sometimes an unexpected stressor or a poorly constructed or maintained sobriety plan will lead to a slip. A slip can be managed and contained by immediate, honest disclosure of the event, followed by a revised plan to shore up your resolve to stop acting out. If you're in a relationship, a slip is something you must tell your spouse or partner about to avoid creating any new secrets. You must disclose your slip no matter the cost. But first discuss it with a therapist, sponsor, or support group friend to take the shame out of it.

Relapse occurs when a sex or love addict is unwilling to be honest about a slip and begins to hide and justify his or her behavior, thereby setting the stage for slips of increasing frequency. Hidden or ongoing slips, lies, isolation, and returning to a secret sexual or romantic life can all define relapse.

During the first few months of my healing process, I was involved in therapy, attended multiple Twelve Step meetings each week, and regularly worked at learning about and managing my problem. I began to pray and meditate, and I opened up to healing. I slowly began to regard my past sexual behavior as a symptom of a difficult time in my life that was now ending. But when I passed the nine-month mark of sobriety, I gradually became less serious about some earlier commitments, such as keeping my Internet filters current and checking in with my sponsor. And I started skipping therapy and going to fewer Twelve Step meetings.

One Saturday when I was feeling overwhelmed from the workweek I thought, "I should really just relax today and take some time for me. I deserve it." So I slept in instead of going to my regular Twelve Step meeting. Then, when my wife went to the grocery store, it occurred to me I could download an app and open it up—just to see how well I was handling my problem. I was only going to look and see who was logged in and then immediately log out, to prove to myself that I now had things under control. Of course, within minutes I'd arranged an online encounter with a total stranger. Afterward, I was shocked at how easily and quickly I seemed to return to my former behaviors. I realized then that unless I consistently and thoroughly followed the plan that had been suggested to me, I wasn't going to get well and stay well.

—Robert, forty-one, chemical engineer

Robert's story demonstrates that having some success in working on sex and love addiction problems can lead to a slip if you convince yourself that you have fixed the problem or are cured. He didn't overtly start out looking for sex, though when reviewing the situation in therapy, he recalled feeling mildly excited about being home alone and feeling entitled to download and open the app.

Warning Signs for Slips and Relapse

- **Overconfidence:** "This has gone really well for a few months. Maybe I have the problem licked. I don't need a therapist anymore."
- **Isolation:** "I will do fine on my own. I don't need to be in constant contact with my recovery or support group, and I don't need to go to those silly meetings every week."
- **Blaming others:** "If my boyfriend hadn't gotten a job that took up so much of his time, I wouldn't be so lonely and tempted by other guys."
- **Making excuses and setting up slippery situations:** "I could leave work with everyone else like I always do, but I think I'm fine now so I will just stay late alone to get this project done."
- **Minimizing a return to problematic situations:** "It's not like I'm talking to other women any more. I'm just looking at a few images. Besides, every guy looks now and then."

- **Ignoring or devaluing feedback from others:** "My Twelve Step group just wants to control me. They are just a bunch of sexually repressed losers. I'm doing fine on my own."
- **Feeling victimized by not having complete sexual freedom:** "Every other guy gets to look at porn as much as he wants. I don't see why I should deprive myself. What's the point in that?"
- **Ignoring previously agreed-upon guidelines:** "That boundary plan doesn't make sense for me when I travel. It really only should be in place when I'm at home."
- **Feeling entitled to return to formerly problematic behaviors:** "Look how hard I've been working at the office and in my recovery. What difference does it make if I look at a few videos here and there? It's not like I have a decent relationship. I deserve something good for me."
- **Using working hard in the healing process to justify acting out sexually:** "I'm not perfect. I'm entitled to have a slip once in a while. I don't have to be a recovery poster child."

If you find yourself in a slip or a relapse, you should immediately check in with your sponsor, reach out to one of the people on your support group phone list, or call your therapist. You've established relationships with these people so they can support you in your day-to-day healing and throw you a lifeline if you fall back into your addiction. Now is the time to utilize that support. Ask for help! It's yourself that you're saving.

CHAPTER TEN

SINGLE PEOPLE AND SEXUAL HEALING: THE DATING CONUNDRUM

After ten years of active sex addiction, here I am in recovery. I'm twenty-seven, and I don't have any sort of sexual or romantic outlet. What am I supposed to do? I don't want to live like a celibate monk the rest of my life, but I don't know how to date or have sex that doesn't involve my computer, my smartphone, and being compulsive. I have no idea how to talk to a woman face-to-face, because all I've ever done is look at porn, have sexual chats on webcams, and hook up for anonymous in-person sex after just a couple of text messages. With all the women I've had sex with, either online or in person, I've never even given out my real name. I don't want to be alone forever, but I'm scared that if I try dating, I'll relapse or just plain make an ass of myself.

—Dion, twenty-seven, truck driver

I feel like I've been on hundreds of dates, maybe even thousands. But were they really dates? Looking back, they feel more like hunting expeditions, with me stalking the guy and seducing him to make him mine, thinking that getting a particular man would fix my life and end my problems. And I pretty much spent my entire life, 24/7, worrying about how I was going to get the next guy—the one who was actually perfect instead of the one that I thought was perfect until I finally hooked him. So even though I have a lot of experience with dating, I

*think I've been doing it totally wrong. I have no idea how to take it
slow, like a normal girl, or how to be emotionally intimate. Do guys
even want that?*

—Celia, thirty-two, store owner

One of the biggest fears expressed by single people entering sex and love
addiction recovery is "What will the rest of my life look like?" They worry
that they'll never have sex again, that they'll never be able to date, and
that they're doomed to a life of either addiction or isolation. Happily, this
is not the case. Instead, healing is about learning to date and be sexual in
healthy, life-affirming ways. As such, there is no reason that any recovering
sex addict who wishes to date and have an active sex life cannot do so. The
only real constraint is that the recovering addict must stay away from the
compulsive sexual and romantic behaviors that were creating negative life
consequences.

ARE YOU READY FOR HEALTHY DATING?

Healing from sex or love addiction does not mean avoiding dating, romance,
or healthy sexual expression. Usually, after you've gotten through the first
six to nine months of active work on your sexual and romantic issues, you
are ready to think about and plan for healthy dating and sexuality. The
safest way to begin this process is by reaching out to those who know you
and help hold you accountable, discussing with them your thoughts, feelings, and desires in regard to dating. These people can help you develop a
written dating plan that, like your sexual boundary plan, provides specific
guidelines that protect your sobriety—outlining how and where to meet
people and how long to date before having sex. After establishing these
boundaries, you are much more likely to make healthy and appropriate
sexual and relationship choices.

Though everyone's dating plan is different, just as everyone's sexual
sobriety plan is different, any dating plan should put you on a path toward
emotional intimacy rather than a return to the intense, sexually charged
behaviors of your addiction.

Moving toward healthy romance and sexuality can be a confusing and imperfect process. Hopefully, before you attempt dating you will have developed a supportive and knowledgeable support network in recovery—people who are available to act as your guides and mentors so you don't have to undertake the dating process alone. If not, then you are probably not ready to start dating. In fact, you should back away from dating and work on building a healthy support network first. It may help if you consider the building of your healthy support network (healthy friendships) as practice for building healthy romantic relationships later on.

The happy news here is that a healthy, sustainable sexual and romantic life for recovering sex addicts does involve both romance and sexuality. The difference from your previous life in addiction is that these new, healthier encounters include a connection beyond the physical.

TAKING IT SLOW

In the early stages of healing, most addicts are fairly clueless about how to create and sustain the kind of healthy intimacy that's needed for a lasting commitment. Nevertheless, many recovering people make the mistake of running out and trying to find a long-term partner the minute they stop acting out. Often, their immediate search for a spouse becomes a means of avoiding emotional challenges, much the same as their acting out behaviors.

Even when marriage or some other form of lifetime commitment is the endgame for you, it is best to not expect that—or even to look for that—right away when you start dating. In all likelihood, you simply don't have the skill set needed to make that happen in a healthy way. Usually, it is better to take things one date at a time, without vesting yourself too much in the outcome of any particular interaction. If things go well and you continue dating someone, that's great. If you end up building an intimate relationship with that person over time, that's even better. But if the other person isn't right for you, or you're not right for him or her, there is no need to take it personally. Just view that person as a practice date, helping to prepare you for the real thing when it eventually comes along.

Basic Guidelines for Dating and Sex in Recovery

Most single people in recovery from sex addiction eventually want to re-engage sexually and romantically with others. If you are among them, there are three dependable rules on which future healthy dating and sexuality depend:

1. You have to get to know the person before you have sex with him or her and really getting to know someone often takes several months.
2. Sex (or romantic intensity) cannot be the primary focus of your encounters. The goal is having fun, not sex.
3. If being with a particular person makes you feel bad—ashamed, used, manipulated, or ignored—before, during, or after a date or sex, then it is a situation you should put a stop to no matter how exciting or attractive that person might be.

These three simple rules provide basic guidelines for avoiding a return to active addiction through dating. By following these rules, you can expect, over time, to see significant changes in your romantic and sexual behavior. Furthermore, these guidelines should form the basis of your written plan for dating in sobriety.

Sexual Fetishes, Sexual Orientation, Sexual Identity, and Sex Addiction

Desiring or engaging in homosexual or bisexual activity, BDSM, the leather scene, cross-dressing, or any other sexual "lifestyle" does not mean you are a sex addict, even if you don't like that these things turn you on. Furthermore, trying to eliminate a part of your arousal template (who or what it is that arouses you) by seeking treatment for sex addiction does not work, and more often than not this tactic is harmful rather than helpful. Put another way, who and what you are attracted to is not related to sexual addiction. Instead, these facets of sexuality are more or less fixed parts of who you are. As such, contemporary research-based therapy encourages people who are unhappy with their arousal template to seek therapy that helps them accept and integrate (rather than deny and try to change) their arousal patterns.

This does not in any way mean that there aren't sex addicts who are also gay, bisexual, or into a fetish. There are. The point we're trying to make here is that unwanted sexual orientation/attraction and sexual addiction are entirely different issues. If you struggle with both unwanted attractions and sexual addiction, as some people do, you will likely require sophisticated, informed therapies that will help you pick these issues apart in a useful way. In such cases, you and your helping professional(s) have the following tasks: 1) Learning everything you can about your arousal patterns; 2) Exploring what is and isn't sexually healthy for you; 3) Finding ways in which you can healthfully integrate your arousal patterns into your life; and 4) Clearly defining and eliminating sexual behavior patterns that are pathological and harmful. The goal is to get a true picture of what is unhealthy versus what is simply unwanted, all the while helping you to move forward toward non-addictive sexuality that aligns with your true sense of self.

Healing from sexual addiction allows for a diverse array of sexual and romantic expression. This means that recovery isn't about what sex addicts might be asked to give up or subtract from their sex life, and it's definitely not about returning to the life they had before seeking help. Instead, sexual recovery is a journey that leads toward a new life in which addicts slowly recover the dignity and self-respect they lost in the shadow-world of active addiction. For some addicts, this is a new concept. One final note here: If you are indeed a sex addict and you want to heal, that means that objectified, non-relational, secretive, and compulsive forms of sexual activity can no longer be a part of your life. Those days need to be done and gone. That said, as long as the way you express your newly evolving sexual self doesn't betray the basic recovery principles of not causing adverse life consequences, not keeping secrets, not being abusive, not causing shame, and not engaging in nonconsensual activities, chances are good that these behaviors are also not going to impede your healing. And if they do, then more work, self-examination and new next steps may be needed. The good news is that there is always a next step when it comes to healthy human sexuality and emotional growth.

HEALTHY DATING USING DIGITAL TECHNOLOGY

It is an unavoidable fact that meeting and dating in the twenty-first century is more often than not facilitated by digital technology. For those who are ready to start looking for a healthy partnership, digital technology provides many avenues to do so, and we encourage using it—even if digital technology also drove your addiction. You just need to proceed cautiously and with a well-thought-out dating plan. To create your dating plan, go to Developing a Dating Plan in the Activity Appendix on page 208. Following are some tips to help you navigate dating while utilizing modern technology.

- Though many social media sites, dating sites, and smartphone apps are not specifically oriented toward sex, overt sexual content can be found pretty much anywhere if you are looking for it. If you find yourself using social media or dating sites and apps to find erotic images or to hook up for anonymous sex, avoid them.
- Some dating sites and apps are specifically geared to single people, whereas others openly offer options for NSHM (not so happily married) people. In fact, some sites and apps are specifically designed for people in committed relationships who are seeking something "on the side." Sites like those should be avoided, as they encourage non-intimate sexual interactions, which is exactly what you are trying to avoid.
- Before you contact or respond to someone, be sure to read that person's profile to see what it is that he or she is seeking. If someone lists "dating and a possible long-term relationship" as an option, that's a good thing. If they list "anonymous sex" as their goal, stay away.
- Go online with a recovering friend present so you are not alone when viewing dating sites.

SAFETY FIRST

It's no secret that digital technology is home to a lot of nefarious people, many of whom cruise social media, dating sites, and smartphone apps in search of potential victims. Basically, these online predators rely on the fact that with only words, photos, and perhaps a short video or two as introduction, a hopeful or emotionally needy person can easily engage in sexualized or romanticized fantasy and "fall for" someone he or she in reality knows very little about.

Dating site/app bad guys generally fall into two categories: sexual predators and financial scammers. The sexual predators romance their potential victims via chats and texts in which they pretend to be the victim's perfect partner. Usually these predators come off as thoughtful, attentive, and flattering. Spinning an intricate web of lies about themselves and their feelings, they build trust and emotional dependency in their victim. Then, when their victim is hooked, they spring the trap, convincing the vulnerable person to meet them at their home or in some remote setting so they can sexually abuse them.

Financial scammers also spend much of their time and effort building trust with potential victims. After they get someone to fall for them, they continue the digital romance until suddenly they need money that only the victim can provide. They prey on that person's natural instinct to help a loved one in need. Often the scammer claims to be traveling in a foreign country on business or on a charity mission and is suddenly in the midst of a medical emergency—for example, the scammer needs emergency surgery that can only be paid for in cash. At that point the victim is asked to wire a large sum of money because the perpetrator's own funds are unavailable for some reason. Another common scam involves the charming foreigner who desperately wants to visit you, but needs money to pay for a plane ticket or visa. You send the money, but your online darling never shows up.

There are a number of things you can do to protect yourself from dating site and hookup app predators. Here are the most imperative actions:

- **Trust your instincts.** If you're feeling uncomfortable, something is wrong. Period. So get out. It doesn't matter how charming and attractive the other person is; if the situation feels "off," it probably is. Remember, under no circumstances are you ever obligated to continue a date or a digital conversation.

- **Always meet in public first.** If you've met someone using digital technology, your initial IRL meetings should take place in a public space such as a coffee shop, café, or mall. You should arrive at the venue on your own, and plan to leave on your own. This way you are less likely to get trapped in someone else's car for a premature make-out session or driven to a location you'd rather not go.

- **Buddy up.** Make sure a close friend or family member knows who you are meeting, when, where, and for how long. Arrange to check in with that person at least once during your date. It's also not unheard of—nor is it impolite—to ask someone to hang out at the venue, discreetly keeping an eye on things from across the room.

- **Go Dutch.** When you initially meet an online companion IRL, both people should pay their own way. If someone you've met online wants money or gifts, walk away. That person does not love you or even care about you. If he or she starts asking for money, alarm bells should be going off. And when alarm bells ring, it's time to leave. If you feel your emotions overriding your instincts, ask your therapist, your sponsor, or a supportive friend in recovery what he or she thinks about the situation.

No matter what, if you are victimized in any way by someone you've met through digital technology, you need to report the abuse. In addition to contacting local authorities, consider turning to one or more of the numerous websites designed to assist people who've been victimized, such as www.haltabuse.org and www.romancescams.org.

Finding the Right Person

The good news here is that dating site/app predators are a small minority of the online population. The vast majority of people seeking to date using digital technology are good people hoping to find the right person. Although online dating absolutely requires you to be on guard for predators, using digital technology to meet and date is, for many, a game changer. Whatever you're seeking—a long-term partner or just someone to date casually while you continue to work on your sex and love addiction issues—there are certain things you can do to raise your odds of success:

- **Be honest.** If you're fifty-five, don't try to pass yourself off as thirty-five. If you post a photo, make sure it's a recent picture that actually looks like you. Face shots only! Don't say that you're a doctor if you're not. And don't say you're looking for a serious relationship if all you're looking for is a few casual "practice" dates.

- **Know what you're looking for, and narrow your search accordingly.** Online dating sites/apps allow you to refine your exploration in a variety of ways, winnowing out people unlikely to appeal to you based on things like location, smoking and drinking status, and education and employment. Select three to five non-appearance-related criteria that are important to you and conduct your search based on those guidelines. After doing this, you can look at the photos of people with whom you have something in common to see which ones you find physically attractive.

- **Pick the right dating site/app.** There are sites and apps for everyone. For example, if you're seeking a long-term relationship, think about a site like eHarmony.com or Match.com. If you're Jewish and want to meet other Jewish people, consider JDate.com. If you're Black and want to meet other African Americans, try BlackPeopleMeet.com.

Remember, the more honest you are about your appearance, what you have to offer, and what it is you're looking for, the more likely you are to find the relationship you seek. The flaws you judge so harshly in yourself may bring joy and fun to someone else. As long as you follow some basic safety and sobriety rules, there is no reason you can't safely and enjoyably locate whatever type of partner you seek, be it a lifetime relationship or something more casual.

CHAPTER ELEVEN

MARRIAGE, LONG-TERM RELATIONSHIPS, AND SEXUAL HEALING: REBUILDING THE BOND

I borrowed my wife's phone one day and saw a few apps I didn't recognize. I clicked on one to find out what it was, and nearly fell over. It was a hookup app, and one of three she was using. She had all sorts of texts and sexts from not just men, but women. It was crazy. I had no idea what she was up to when I was at work. She came clean about the hookups and affairs, and I figured for sure our relationship was over. But now it's a year later and we're still together. Things aren't perfect, but she's been doing what she needs to do, and I've been doing the things that I need to do to take care of myself, and I think we're going to make it. Our relationship will never be like it was before I found out about her love addiction, but maybe that's not such a bad thing.

—Joseph, thirty-three, computer technician

My husband would stay up late at night, after I went to bed, almost every evening. He told me he was playing video games with his online friends. Well, he was, sort of. Just not the sort of games I thought, and not with the sort of friends that I thought. I only found out about his cheating when I got up to go to the bathroom one night and found him masturbating on a webcam with another woman. It was horrible. We had a huge fight and I told him to leave. But after I cooled down we agreed to counseling before I made any big decisions. Luckily, our therapist knew about cybersex addiction. Now my husband is in recovery and doing what he's supposed to be doing. I don't completely trust him yet, but in my support group everyone tells me this is normal, that if he continues to be honest about what he's doing (and not doing), my distrust and my anger will go away over time.

—Lisa, twenty-eight, assistant professor

HEALING BROKEN TRUST

Most sex and love addicts have lied, covered up, manipulated, and hidden their secret lives. No wonder their loved ones feel betrayed and violated, finding trust difficult if not impossible in their relationships. Even when the recovering addict adheres to a strict program, studies have shown that it often takes a year or more before the betrayed partner ceases to have doubts about the addict's activities. Complicating matters is the fact that sex addicts, just like drug addicts and alcoholics, sometimes relapse, often multiple times. When this happens, it becomes much more difficult for the relationship to survive and thrive, though healing, rebuilding trust, and establishing new emotional intimacy are still possible.

A 2012 study of ninety-two partners of recovering sex addicts who had slipped or relapsed at least once looked at the cheated-on partners' initial experience of learning about the acting out, the effect of the addict's slip or relapse on the relationship, and reasons the cheated-on partners decided to stay in or leave the relationship.[1] One significant finding was that betrayed partners usually learned about slips and relapses on their own rather than hearing about them from the addict. Over half of the betrayed partners said their relationship worsened after they learned about the slip or relapse. However, there was a significant difference in their response to discovery versus disclosure: Those partners who discovered the acting out before the addict disclosed it almost universally reported worse relational outcomes. And much of the time, honesty on the part of the addict was an important factor in the betrayed partner's choosing to stay rather than end the relationship. When the betrayed partners were asked to list the reasons they might leave the relationship in the future, another relapse was, as expected, the most common reason. The number two reason was dishonesty. So it appears that the best course of action for a recovering sex addict who wants to save his or her relationship involves being honest. Indeed, the most effective way to rebuild trust and save a relationship is for the addict to be consistently honest, difficult as that may be.

Recovering sex addicts must realize that the original relationship trust they had is now long gone and cannot ever be regained. The addict destroyed it with his or her behavior. This means that the addict is no longer an equal partner in the relationship. To regain an equal footing, the addict must build and earn a new foundation of trust. This is key to the survival of the relationship, and the addict must earn such trust by being rigorously honest.

ADVICE FOR THE RECOVERING ADDICT

Recovering sex or love addicts who hope to make things right in their relationship need to recognize early on that they are rightfully in the doghouse. Usually, getting out of the doghouse involves the following behaviors and attitudes:

- Listening and reflecting rather than reacting
- Listening with the context of the past hurts in mind
- Being non-defensive
- Being grateful and expressing humility
- Not assuming your partner will see your point or understand
- Not expecting a "gold star" for meeting minimum relationship requirements
- Finding recovering people to meet your healthy needs and not demanding that your spouse meet them

Following are some specific things you can do, as a recovering sex addict, to rebuild trust and healthy intimacy in your relationship:

- Exhibiting rigorous honesty with everyone close to you in both small and large issues
- Working toward greater empathy and insight into the pain you have caused your partner and loved ones
- Allowing your partner time to rebuild trust, letting him or her feel anger and mistrust without you expecting an immediate "all is forgiven"
- Avoiding apologies, gift giving in hopes of forgiveness, and making excuses for past behavior, and understanding that simply acknowledging what you have done and not repeating it is more effective than a thousand attempts at "I'm sorry"
- Spending time with your partner doing things he or she enjoys, like going to a movie your partner wants to see, or to an art show, or to a baseball game, or whatever—as long as the action demonstrates that what matters to your partner also matters to you
- Establishing and maintaining a stable and consistent plan for your own self-care
- Remaining committed to your clear plan for recovery and long-term behavior change

Advice for the Betrayed Partner

The onus of saving a damaged relationship is not entirely on the sex or love addict. The betrayed spouse needs to step up, too, to try to understand what part (if any) he or she had in the loss of relationship trust. If you are the betrayed partner of a sex addict, here are some steps you may want to consider:

- Let yourself be angry and hurt—you've earned it!
- Educating yourself about addiction—reading, taking classes, going to support groups

- Committing to your own personal healing and self-care
- Working toward being less judgmental and less critical by showing a greater willingness to acknowledge your part in your challenges as a couple
- Being willing, over time, to grow beyond anger and betrayal and to find a path toward trust

A Few Words About Rigorous Honesty

The best antidote for a past life of secrecy and dishonesty is a present life of rigorous honesty in all areas, small and large. It takes many days, weeks, and months of consistency in this regard to overcome the distrust you've created in your relationship. Simple things are very meaningful when trying to re-establish trust. For example, if you are going to be late, even a little, phone or text your partner to explain. If you agree to pick up some milk on the way home but forget, it is better to admit that you forgot than to make up some excuse. If you need to use the computer at home, it is better to have it in a high-traffic area than to sit behind a closed door, expecting your partner to "just trust you" and to believe that nothing inappropriate is going on. Most of all, willingly allow your partner to install filtering and accountability software on your computer, laptop, tablet, smartphone, and any other digital devices you use. This will not only help you stay sober, it will help you to rebuild relationship trust.

Regaining trust in my husband has been a gradual process. He's been very trustworthy since he started recovery. He makes sure to be home when he is supposed to be home, and he's made himself available by phone at all times, even if I call him several times a day. He always phones me or leaves a note if he has a change of plans. He will sit listening without argument, sometimes for long periods, when I need to express my anger and disappointment, even though I know he wants to defend himself. For a long time he has stayed on the straight and narrow, even if he has to go out of his way. It's taken about a year, but I find that I don't need all of that accountability anymore. If he is going to be late, he doesn't have to phone to let me know why; I am no longer sitting at home tapping my fingers and wondering where he is if he is five minutes overdue.

—Nancy, forty, wife of a recovering sex addict

In short, it is essential for the partners of sex addicts to see the recovering addict fully engaged in active healing through regular attendance at Twelve Step meetings, therapy, spiritual work, honesty, accountability, and consistent adherence to the safe, non-addictive use of digital technology. Ongoing behavior of this sort shows the betrayed partner that there is sincerity and commitment to moving past previous problems and changing problematic behaviors permanently.

ESCHEWING THE QUICK FIX

Some couples who want to restore intimacy in their relationships will turn to sexual intensity or romantic "honeymoon" experiences, trying to quickly re-create some closeness following the disclosure of a sex addict's problem. This is a fairly normal response. Unfortunately, while sexual and romantic intensity may feel good in the moment and provide each partner with a measure of reassurance, sex used as a means to soothe difficult feelings enables both partners to avoid deeper, more troubling issues.

It is much healthier, though usually much less comfortable, to engage in a cooling off period. This involves a mutual agreement to not cycle into sexual or romantic intensity and to put off any longer-term decisions (like whether to break up or permanently change residences) until there is more clarity about where things are headed. It's essential to take some time— usually anywhere from thirty to ninety days—to grieve the past, to learn more about addiction and addictive patterns of behavior, and to work on honest modes of communication and healing through support groups, couples counseling, and individual therapies before making any major relationship decisions. After this period of focused recovery and healing, it's more likely that decisions about the relationship will be made with careful consideration.

EMPATHY

The process of healing requires each partner to develop greater empathy for the other. Empathy is the ability to feel and relate deeply to what someone else is going through, even if you have not had the very same experience. Going to couples counseling and attending support group meetings with other individuals and couples will help facilitate this process. Sometimes it can be easier for the addict to empathize when hearing the pain of someone else's partner than when confronted by his or her own partner's pain. And ultimately, when betrayed partners feel that their pain is understood, they are more likely to believe that the addict will not hurt them again.

Similarly, partners of sex addicts are often focused on their own hurt, betrayal, and injured self-esteem, for which they blame the addict. Understandably, they fail to see that giving up the acting out is a real loss that their addicted spouse will need time to grieve and work through. They are appropriately angry and often judgmental as well, seeing the one who acted out as the only one with a problem and themselves as innocent victims. This often adds to the addict's feelings of shame and low self-esteem. Counseling, listening exercises, role-playing in therapy sessions, and listening to others when they tell their stories can all help to build empathy and to melt away judgmental thinking in the betrayed partner.

I'm a critical care nurse, and my career is very demanding—more so after I got promoted to head nurse of the cardiac care unit. Right around the same time that happened, Paul, my husband of twenty-five years, retired and got interested in surfing the Net on his laptop. In the mid-1990s, he had a number of affairs that I found out about, and he entered treatment for his sex addiction. He'd been sexually sober and faithful ever since, and I really thought we were past it all. But suddenly he was staying up late on his computer. And after a couple of months, he seemed to lose interest in sex with me. At first I blamed this on my new work schedule and that fact that I was worn out a lot of the time. Eventually, though, he admitted he'd been looking at porn and having webcam sex with women he met online.

He immediately went back to his Twelve Step program for sex addiction, setting up guidelines for computer and smartphone use and asking me to install filtering and accountability software on all of his digital devices. At first I was furious, but later I realized that some of our marital issues were my fault. Because I had become preoccupied with work, Paul felt unneeded and unappreciated, which was not good for our marriage. We started going to counseling together, and we committed to daily time sitting and talking with each other, plus weekly dates and spending more time together on my days off. Because of this, our relationship has evolved and we've actually built a level of intimacy that we've never had before.

—Jessie, fifty, critical care nurse

The experience of Jessie and Paul is not unusual. Many couples negatively affected by sex addiction are able, through effort and hard work in counseling and elsewhere, to not only stay together but to build a stronger, happier, and more loving relationship than ever. If you and your partner are willing to put in the effort, you can too.

ACTION STEPS FOR RELATIONSHIP SURVIVAL

Not all recovering sex and love addicts are single. Many are married or otherwise partnered, and nearly always their relationships have been seriously damaged by their sexual and romantic acting out. If this is the case for you, then you and your partner will need to learn how to nurture not only yourselves as individuals but also each other and your relationship. The following are action steps that couples can take toward reconnection after the initial rage, grief, and pain of the initial betrayal have become less immediate (often 6–9 months).

Make "Dates" for Time Together. In our busy lives it can be incredibly easy to let time slip away without ever setting aside a few moments for our relationship. The distractions of work, family, kids, friends, and even recovery from addiction can easily take precedence. Yet studies have proven the need for couples to spend time together without distractions. This is especially true for couples healing from the pain of sexual and romantic betrayals. Although making advance preparations often seems unromantic, it is essential that couples plan for and set aside specific times to be together. The goal here is to make actual dates—unbreakable except in an emergency—for play and relaxation, with or without sex. Whether it's a trip to the beach or an evening on the town, all couples (especially those whose relationship is damaged and struggling) need time away from the stress of day-to-day life if they want to experience healthy growth and intimacy.

Listen. One tool that helps couples grow closer is listening. Learning more effective ways to listen to one another and making time for sharing is essential. Try out this fifteen to twenty minute exercise when the distractions of the day have ended. You and your partner sit facing each other. Each person has five minutes of uninterrupted time to say whatever he or she wants to the other person. Each person should feel completely free to speak about his or her day, feelings, work, and family. Then the other partner takes a turn, spending five minutes speaking without interruption. The last five to ten minutes are a time to discuss what each partner has heard and how he or she feels about it. Carried out two to three times weekly, this simple exercise goes a long way toward helping couples (re)establish intimacy and closeness.

Share Activities. Couples who are actively seeking to heal need to find time for activities that stimulate and interest both of them. Hiking, gardening, playing sports, going to museums, and shopping at antique stores are all examples of potential relationship-enhancing activities. Experiences that take the couple out of their daily routine result in bonding and shared intimacy the likes of which no therapy session can even hope to offer.

Practice Nonsexual Touching and Holding. Many people who have issues with sexual or romantic behaviors grew up in homes where they had very little touch and experienced little physical intimacy, or they had childhoods where their exposure to intimacy was inappropriate and overwhelming. To overcome this, recovering couples need to work on building physical closeness that is not necessarily focused on sex. Hand-holding, hugs, cuddling, massages, shoulder rubs, and kisses all offer warmth and validation that cannot be gained from words alone.

(Re)Introduce Romance. As a couple moves toward forgiveness and healing, romantic interactions can help. This does not necessarily mean sex. Rather, we are talking about the actions people take to help each other feel loved and appreciated. Notes, cards, flowers, unexpected compliments, and surprise gifts all build intimacy. These activities are best carried out in the later stages of healing, as opposed to early in the process when they might be viewed as a desperate attempt to buy forgiveness.

CHAPTER TWELVE

MOVING BEYOND THE PROBLEM

I have accepted that I abuse pornography in the same way that other people abuse drugs or gambling. I tried to stop on my own many times, but I never managed it for more than a day or two. Now I am seeking help, as my addiction has jeopardized my marriage and my family life, as well as my career. I started by seeing a therapist, who questioned me about my anxiety, which is what I thought my problem was. She was smart enough to realize that the anxiety I was talking about was more a symptom than an underlying issue and that my real problem was that my coping mechanism—escaping into pornography—was out of control and causing all sorts of problems. She referred me to a specialist in sex addiction and I started treatment with him, which included individual sessions, group sessions with other porn-addicted men, and Twelve Step meetings. As of now, I've been away from porn and other forms of online sexuality for over two years, and I feel great. My marriage is stronger than ever, and I'm much more "together" with other aspects of my life.

—Dave, forty-eight, journalist

Cybersex problems don't just come from having a computer or smartphone. I can see now that I had issues with sexual and romantic fantasy long before I discovered the Internet and hookup apps. But once I got online, I suddenly had access to the biggest singles bar in the whole world, and I could go there any time I wanted in what felt like total safety. In the digital world it was easy to approach people I was interested in and to walk away from those I wasn't interested in. And if someone rejected me, it didn't matter very much because they weren't "real" and there was always another option. The problem was that I forgot about my real life. The allure and the excitement of online romances were just stronger than my need to go to work, pay rent, buy groceries, and take care of myself. Over time, my life gradually fell apart until I was completely alone and desperate. Eventually my siblings stepped in and forced me to get help. I am so glad they did. Now I have a job that I like and a nice apartment, and I've even started dating. I haven't met the right guy for me, but that's okay. I'm probably not ready for a serious romance anyway. But someday I will be, thanks to my recovery.

—Anna, thirty-seven, speech therapist

There is more to healing than simply stopping a problem behavior. The word "recovery" is used in addiction treatment because it implies your sense of self, life, and creativity are nurtured and cultivated. Although the "do's" of the recovery process discussed in the last several chapters are the tools that bring about and help maintain change, more must be done to ensure lasting happiness and peace of mind. True long-term healing occurs through a commitment to the practice of self-care, and by learning how to find and enjoy the healthy pleasures that make life worthwhile.

THE IMPORTANCE OF SELF-NURTURING

People with addictive problems often have difficulty taking time out to care for themselves, or even recognizing that they should. For instance, sex and love addicts tend to be intensity-focused rather than self-soothing and self-care focused. Unable to be soothed by long-term meaningful life rewards such as watching the garden grow or developing intimacy in a close partnership, these people leach intensity from external events and experiences for distraction and dissociation. This is the essence of their problem.

Sex addicts use sexual and/or romantic fantasies and behaviors to avoid feelings of emptiness and inner discomfort. When they enter recovery, these feelings must be relieved through self-care and self-nurturing. Thus, long-term healing includes learning how to "do nothing" for periods of time, along with finding and developing healthy hobbies and interests. This part of the process can be so foreign to those healing from sexual or romantic addiction that it ends up being the hardest part of recovery.

NURTURING TASKS FOR THE RECOVERING ADDICT

Attend to Nonsexual Friendships. Sex addicts who are active in their addiction often have very little going on in their personal lives beyond the addictive behaviors. Absorption in their sexual or romantic fantasy life prevents them from being aware of any loneliness or isolation they might otherwise feel. Even if they are active socially and appear to be close to others, they feel separated by their secrets and the all-consuming nature of their behaviors. Those who are aware of the problematic nature of their sexual and romantic activities often feel too embarrassed to talk about it with friends and other supportive people, and instead remain isolated and unhappy.

Isolation is a hallmark of emotional disease. Every healing person needs others besides partners and immediate family members with whom they can discuss their painful challenges and losses. This is why participation in group therapy, Twelve Step recovery programs, and other support groups is encouraged. Even though it may be embarrassing at first to discuss such concerns, the support and acceptance that come with reaching out to safe people can far outweigh any discomfort.

Meditate. Long encouraged by religious groups and Twelve Step programs, the practice of regular meditation can create more peace and calm within. If the goal is to move away from intensity and arousal as a source of distraction, then working to create calm and peace within is a smart step. Taking classes or finding a good book about meditation is the easiest way to start. Suggested books include *Mindfulness in Plain English*, by Bhante Henepola Gunaratana, *Wherever You Go, There You Are,* by Jon Kabat-Zinn, and the anonymously written *Answers in the Heart: Daily Meditations for Men and Women Recovering from Sexual Addiction.*

Physical Fitness. Those who intensely pursue instant gratification through sex usually neglect their physical health and utilize few healthy methods to reduce everyday stressors. This is why addiction treatment programs typically include physical fitness regimens as an important element of their work. Achieving life balance means paying attention to your emotional, spiritual, *and physical* health. Aside from all the benefits of physical self-care and weight loss, exercise induces many of the same neurochemical changes in the brain that are produced by intensity-based addictive behaviors such as sexual acting out and compulsive romantic intrigue—only in a much healthier fashion. Even the simplest exercise routine, such as walking, when used consistently and in a committed fashion, will add significantly to feelings of serenity, peace, and contentment.

Find Balance. The pressures of our modern world make it easy for anyone's life to get out of balance, especially those who have relied on sexual or romantic fantasies and behaviors to distract themselves from "life as it happens." Over time, too much attention goes to the addictive behaviors and not enough goes to friends, romantic partners, family, children, or the demands of work. Life turns into a frantic attempt to put out fires and play catch-up with commitments that have been ignored at work and at home in favor of acting out. Much of the time, life is lived "in overwhelm."

When overwhelmed, the active addict's handiest solution was always more intensity through acting out. The healthy solution for addicts in recovery, however, is to set appropriate priorities and boundaries for work commitments, self-care, and personal relationships. Establish a plan for the maximum number of hours you will work each week, and prioritize commitments to family, friends, and personal time. This will go a long way toward helping you attain and maintain balance and a sense of control in your life.

Spend Time in Nature. Feelings of isolation and aloneness are often pervasive for those who abuse sex and romance. Sometimes, cybersex addicts have felt alone their whole lives. A powerful way of realizing that you are not alone, but rather a part of a vast universe, is to spend some time in nature. Outdoors, the interconnectedness of life is realized. A visit to Mount St. Helens in the northwest United States, for example, makes clear both the devastation a volcanic eruption can have and the regeneration that is possible. A trip to the Grand Canyon shows how, over vast amounts of time, water can carve a huge rift in solid rock. Closer to home perhaps, a walk in the woods illustrates how birds depend on trees to build their nests, on worms to feed their offspring, and on their partner to incubate their eggs. Any trip into the wilderness shows us that interdependence, not isolation, is the rule of nature. And this is a very helpful rule for recovering people to see, internalize, and put into practice.

Lonely? Get a Pet. Medical studies have shown that older people with pets are happier, healthier, and live longer than people who don't share their lives with animals. When asked to give an example of unconditional love, many people immediately think of the way a dog or cat loves its owner. Indeed, pets can immeasurably enhance the lives of their owners. Having a dog or cat or some other friendly animal to greet you at the door when coming home from work, keep you company when reading or watching TV, or entice you out of the house for a walk can help to keep "alone" from becoming "lonely," especially for people who live by themselves. Moreover, caring for the physical and emotional needs of another living being, whether human or animal, can provide a different focus to life besides just worrying about oneself.

Engage in Hobbies, Sports, Games, and "Having Fun." When deeply engaged in the recovery process, it is easy to become so focused on Twelve Step meetings, therapy sessions, work, quality time with the kids, and other previously neglected goal-oriented activities that recreation is forgotten about or avoided. When life becomes busy and complex, taking time out for travel, hobbies, sports, and other "nonproductive" activities may seem silly. However, recharging your battery with fun activities provides the self-nurturing that makes you ready to go out and succeed at work, relationships, and other aspects of life. The key to a productive and psychologically healthy lifestyle is to incorporate play and recreation in whatever dose is necessary to keep your life in balance.

Create a "Home" at Home. When sexual and romantic fantasies and behaviors are your primary life priority, there is little room to focus on creating a home life that is warm and inviting. Though sex addicts use the intensity of their behaviors as a way to ignore their emotional or "inner" selves, they also ignore their outside environment. In recovery, take the time to put in a garden, paint a guest room, buy flowers, or rearrange the furniture. The simple acts of improving your home and taking daily or weekly steps to maintain it reflect an important commitment to taking care of yourself, which in turn provides an ongoing reminder of the positive changes that sobriety can bring.

LAST WORDS

While for some people sexual activity and romance provide a path to enjoyment, play, and healthy stimulation, there are many who use these activities compulsively, finding over time that these normally healthy distractions are destructive to their beliefs, self-esteem, and relationships. Yes, most who find sexnology problematic for any reason are able to simply avoid it, keeping it out of their personal lives and relationships. However, there are people who lose the ability to choose when or even if they will use digital technology for sexual and/or romantic purposes. For these people and those close to them, engaging with sexual images, videos, stories, text and video chat, virtual sex, dating sites, social media, and hookup apps brings confusion, distance, and feelings of hopelessness that can feel irresolvable.

This book has discussed the consequences of sex and love addiction, and described the steps that those caught up in compulsive sexuality and romance can take in order to rebuild healthy lives. By doing this, we have tried to offer information and most of all hope to those who have lost parts of their lives and spirit to this problem of isolation and loneliness. Like those who abuse or are addicted to substances, people who find themselves or those they love tangled in the web of tech-driven sexual or romantic addiction may feel hopeless and helpless. If you are among these people, take heart, because you have taken the first step toward hope and help by reading this book.

Over the last several decades, tens of thousands of sex addicts have found help and healing by following the steps outlined herein—recognizing their problem, going to a knowledgeable therapist, becoming involved in self-help groups, setting appropriate boundaries, rebuilding their relationships, and restoring balance in their lives. To begin, all that is required is the willingness to be honest, ask for help, and get well.

We wish you all the best in your journey.

RESOURCES

RESOURCES
FOR ADDICTS

SEX AND LOVE ADDICTION RESOURCES

General Information

- The Sexual Recovery Institute website (www.sexualrecovery.com) has extensive information about dealing with and healing from cybersex addiction, love addiction, and other intimacy disorders.
- The American Association of Sexuality Educators, Counselors, and Therapists website (aasect.org) offers a great deal of useful information for cybersex addicts.
- The Association for the Treatment of Sexual Abusers website (www.atsa.com) offers useful information about sexual abuse.
- The Ben Franklin Institute offers, live, online, and DVD trainings that can be accessed via their website (bfisummit.com). Much of author Rob Weiss's material has been recorded by them and is available for purchase.
- Gentle Path Press (www.gentlepath.com) publishes books, workbooks, and videos on sexual addiction and recovery.
- The International Institute for Trauma & Addiction Professionals (www.sexhelp.com) has contact information for therapists, listed by state, who are certified as CSATs (Certified Sex Addiction Therapists).

185

- The Safer Society Foundation website (www.safersociety.org) offers useful information on sexual abuse.
- The Society for the Advancement of Sexual Health website (www.sash. net) provides contact information for knowledgeable therapists, listed by city and state, as well as information about upcoming sex addiction conferences and training events.

Sexual Addiction Books

- Anonymous, *Answers in the Heart: Daily Meditations for Men and Women Recovering from Sex Addiction.* (Center City, MN: Hazelden, 1989).
- Anonymous, *Sex Addicts Anonymous.* (New York: Sex Addicts Anonymous, 2009).
- Anonymous, *Sex and Love Addicts Anonymous.* (New York: The Augustine Fellowship, 1986).
- B. Schaeffer, *Is It Love or Is It Addiction? (Third Edition).* (Center City, MN: Hazelden, 2009).
- P. Carnes, *Out of the Shadows: Understanding Sex Addiction.* (Center City, MN: Hazelden, 2001).
- P. Carnes, *Contrary to Love: Helping the Sexual Addict.* (Center City, MN: Hazelden, 1994).
- P. Carnes, *Don't Call it Love: Recovery from Sex Addiction.* (New York: Bantam, 1992).
- G. Collins and A. Adleman, *Breaking the Cycle: Free Yourself from Sex Addiction, Porn Obsession, and Shame.* (Oakland, CA: New Harbinger Publications, 2011).
- M.D. Corley and J. Schneider, *Disclosing Secrets: An Addict's Guide to What, to Whom, and How Much to Reveal.* (N. Charleston, SC: CreateSpace, 2012).
- M. Ferree, *No Stones: Women Redeemed from Sexual Addiction.* (Downer's Grove, IL: IVP Books, 2010).

- W. Maltz and L. Maltz, *The Porn Trap: The Essential Guide to Overcoming Problems Caused By Pornography.* (New York: HarperCollins, 2008).
- K. McDaniel, *Ready to Heal: Breaking Free of Addictive Relationships.* (Carefree, AZ: Gentle Path Press, 2012).
- R. Weiss, *Sex Addiction 101: A Basic Guide to Healing from Sex, Porn, and Love Addiction.* (Long Beach, CA: Elements Behavioral Health, 2013).
- R. Weiss, *Cruise Control: Understanding Sex Addiction in Gay Men (Second Edition).* (Carefree, AZ: Gentle Path Press, 2013).

Twelve Step Groups

- Sex Addicts Anonymous (SAA), 800-477-8191; 713-869-4902, saa-recovery.org/
- Sex and Love Addicts Anonymous (SLAA), 210-828-7900, www.slaafws.org/
- Sexaholics Anonymous (SA), 866-424-8777, www.sa.org/
- Sexual Compulsives Anonymous (SCA), 800-977-HEAL, www.sca-recovery.org/
- Sexual Recovery Anonymous (SRA), www.sexualrecovery.org/

RESOURCES FOR OTHER ADDICTIONS

General Information

- www.mayoclinic.org/diseases-conditions/compulsive-gambling/basics/definition/con-20023242 offers great information about **compulsive gambling**—what it is, how to recognize it, how it can be treated, and so on.

- Useful information on **compulsive spending** can be found at www.ncbi.nlm.nih.gov/pmc/articles/PMC1805733/.
- Useful information on **digital and online video game addiction** can be found at www.video-game-addiction.org.
- Useful information about all types of **eating disorders** can be found on the National Eating Disorders Association website at www.nationaleatingdisorders.org/.
- General information about **substance abuse and mental health** can be found on the Substance Abuse and Mental Health Services Administration website at www.samhsa.gov/.
- General information on **substance abuse** can be found on the National Council on Alcoholism and Drug Dependence website at www.ncadd.org/.
- General information on **substance abuse** can be found on the National Institute on Drug Abuse website at www.drugabuse.gov/.
- **Substance abuse** treatment information can be found at www.promises.com.
- **Substance abuse** treatment information can be found at www.recoveryranch.com.
- **Substance abuse** treatment information can be found at www.elementsbehavioralhealth.com/treatment.

Other Addiction Books

- C. Costin and G.S. Grabb, *8 Keys to Recovery from an Eating Disorder: Effective Strategies from Therapeutic Practice and Personal Experience.* (New York: WW Norton & Co, 2011).
- O. Ogas and S. Gaddam, *A Billion Wicked Thoughts: What the Internet Tells Us About Sexual Relationships.* (New York: Penguin, 2012).
- Anonymous, *Alcoholics Anonymous.* (New York: AA World Services).
- T. Schulman, *Bought Out and Spent! Recovery from Compulsive Shopping and Spending.* (West Conshohocken, PA: Infinity Publishing, 2008).

- H. Shaffer, *Change Your Gambling, Change Your Life: Strategies for Managing Your Gambling and Improving Your Finances, Relationships, and Health.* (San Francisco, CA: Josey-Bass, 2012).
- J. Allen, *Coping with Trauma: Hope Through Understanding.* (New York: Amer Psychiatric Pub, 2004).
- K.J. Roberts, *Cyber Junkie: Escape the Gaming and Internet Trap.* (Center City, MN: Hazelden, 2010).
- B. Brown, *Daring Greatly: How the Courage to Be Vulnerable Transforms the Way We Live, Love, Parent, and Lead.* (New York: Penguin, 2012).
- P. Carnes, S. Carnes, and J. Bailey, *Facing Addiction: Starting Recovery from Alcohol and Drugs.* (Carefree, AZ: Gentle Path Press, 2011).
- D.M. Ruiz, *The Four Agreements: A Practical Guide to Personal Freedom.* (San Rafael, CA: Amber-Allen Publishing, 1997).
- P. Carnes, *A Gentle Path through the Twelve Steps: A Guide for All People in the Process of Recovery.* (Center City, MN: Hazelden, 2013).
- B. Brown, *The Gifts of Imperfection: Let Go of Who You Think You're Supposed to Be and Embrace Who You Are.* (Center City, MN: Hazelden, 2010).
- M. Lancelot, *Gripped by Gambling.* (Tucson, AZ: Wheatmark, 2007).
- J. Poppink, *Healing Your Hungry Heart: Recovering from Your Eating Disorder.* (San Francisco, CA: Conari, 2011).
- A. Doan, B. Strickland, and D. Gentile, *Hooked on Games: The Lure and Cost of Video Game and Internet Addiction.* (FEP International, 2012).
- B. Brown. *I Thought It Was Just Me (but it isn't): Making the Journey from "What Will People Think?" to "I Am Enough."* (New York: Penguin Putman, 2008).
- Anonymous. *Living Sober.* (New York: AA World Services, 2002).
- D. Griffin, *A Man's Way through the Twelve Steps.* (Center City, MN: Hazelden, 2009).
- J. Ortberg, *The Me I Want to Be: Becoming God's Best Version of You.* (Grand Rapids, MI: Zondervan, 2010).
- Anonymous, *Narcotics Anonymous.* (New York: AA World Services, 2008).

- R. Ladouceur and S. Lachance, *Overcoming Your Pathological Gambling: Workbook.* (New York: Oxford University Press, 2008).
- S. Palaian, *Spent: Break the Buying Obsession and Discover Your True Worth.* (Center City, MN: Hazelden, 2009).
- A. Benson, *To Buy or Not to Buy: Why We Overshop, and How to Stop.* (Boston, MA: Trumpeter Books, 2008).
- C. Courtois and J. Ford, *Treatment of Complex Trauma: A Sequenced, Relationship-Based Approach.* (New York: Guilford, 2012).
- Anonymous, *Twelve Steps and Twelve Traditions.* (New York: AA World Services, 2002).
- Anonymous, *Twenty Four Hours a Day.* (Center City, MN: Hazelden, 1954).
- S. Covington, *A Woman's Way through the Twelve Steps* (Center City, MN: Hazelden, 1994).
- B. Brown, *Women & Shame: Reaching Out, Speaking Truths and Building Connection.* (Austin, TX: 3C Press, 2004).

Twelve Step Support Groups

- Alcoholics Anonymous, 212-870-3400, www.aa.org
- Clutterers Anonymous, 866-402-6685, www.clutterersanonymous.org
- Cocaine Anonymous, 800-347-8998, www.ca.org
- Crystal Meth Anonymous, 855-638-4383, www.crystalmeth.org
- Debtors Anonymous, 800-421-2383, www.debtorsanonymous.org
- Emotions Anonymous, 651-647-9712, www.emotionsanonymous.org
- Food Addicts Anonymous, 772-878-9657, www.foodaddictsanonymous.org
- Food Addicts in Recovery Anonymous, 781-932-6300, www.foodaddicts.org
- Gamblers Anonymous, 213-386-8789, www.gamblersanonymous.org
- Marijuana Anonymous, 800-766-6779, www.marijuana-anonymous.org
- Narcotics Anonymous, 818-773-9999, www.na.org

- Nicotine Anonymous, www.nicotine-anonymous.org
- On-Line Gamers Anonymous, www.olganon.org
- Overeaters Anonymous, 505-891-2664, www.oa.org
- Pills Anonymous, www.pillsanonymous.org
- Spenders Anonymous, www.spenders.org
- Survivors of Incest Anonymous, 410-282-3400, www.siawso.org
- Underearners Anonymous, www.underearnersanonymous.org
- Workaholics Anonymous, www.workaholics-anonymous.org

RESOURCES FOR SPOUSES AND FAMILIES OF ADDICTS

General Information

- Useful information for partners of alcoholics and drug addicts can be found at Addiction Treatment Magazine website www.addictiontreatmentmagazine.com/addiction/drug-addiction/how-to-deal-with-your-partners-drug-abuse/.
- Useful information on codependency can be found at www.nmha.org/go/codependency.

Books for Spouses

- M. Beattie, *Codependents' Guide to the Twelve Steps.* (New York: Touchstone, 1992).
- M. Beattie, *Codependent No More: How to Stop Controlling Others and Start Caring for Yourself.* (Center City, MN: Hazelden, 1986).
- P. Carnes, D. Laaser, and M. Laaser, *Open Hearts: Renewing Relationships with Recovery, Romance, and Reality.* (Carefree, AZ: Gentle Path Press, 1990).
- S. Carnes, *Mending a Shattered Heart: A Guide for Partners of Sex Addicts.* (Carefree, AZ: Gentle Path Press, 2011).
- S. Carnes, M. Lee, and A. Rodriguez, *Facing Heartbreak: Steps to Recovery for Partners of Sex Addicts.* (Carefree, AZ: Gentle Path Press, 2012).

- P. Collins and G. Collins, *A Couple's Guide to Sexual Addiction: A Step-by-Step Plan to Rebuild Trust and Restore Intimacy.* (New York: Harper & Row, 2011).
- J. Schneider and M.D. Corley, *Surviving Disclosure: A Partner's Guide for Healing and the Betrayal of Intimate Trust.* (N. Charleston, SC: CreateSpace, 2012).
- D. Kaplan, *For Love and Money: Exploring Sexual & Financial Betrayal in Relationships.* (N. Charleston, SC: CreateSpace, 2013).
- P. Mellody, A.W. Miller, and J.K. Miller, *Facing Codependence: What It Is, Where It Comes From, How It Sabotages Our Lives.* (New York, Harper & Row, 1989).
- J. Schneider and B. Schneider, *Sex, Lies, and Forgiveness (Third Edition).* (Tucson, AZ: Recovery Resources Press, 2004).
- J. Schneider, *Back from Betrayal: Recovering from his Affairs (Third Edition).* (Tucson, AZ: Recovery Resources Press, 2005).

Twelve Step Groups

- Adult Children of Alcoholics, 562-595-7831, www.adultchildren.org
- Al-Anon, 800-344-2666, al-anon.alateen.org
- Alateen (ages twelve to seventeen), 800-356-9996, al-anon.alateen.org
- Co-Anon, 520-513-5028, www.co-anon.org
- Co-Dependents Anonymous, 602-277-7991, www.coda.org
- Co-Dependents of Sex Addicts, 866-899-2672, www.cosa-recovery.org
- Families Anonymous, 800-736-9805, www.familiesanonymous.org
- S-Anon, 800-210-8141, 615-833-3152, www.sanon.org
- Recovering Couples Anonymous, 877-663-2317, www.recovering-couples.org

RESOURCES FOR THERAPISTS

General Information

Not all therapists are well-suited to treating sex addicts. Some may simply be uncomfortable with the explicit nature of the problem. Others, lacking training in CBT and other structured, accountability-based treatment methodologies can be dismissive or simply uncomfortable with making contracts, giving homework, and doing the required confrontation with distortions and denial. Still others see sex addicts as perpetrators rather than damaged individuals in need of assistance. There is nothing wrong with or bad about any of this. No internist feels bad because he or she has to refer someone to a bone specialist; the internist just makes the referral in the patient's best interest. It is no different in the therapy world. None of us has to treat or knows how to treat every client no matter what.

The reality here is that people who compulsively abuse digital technology for sexual and/or romantic purposes need therapists who specifically and intuitively understand addiction treatment and how that knowledge and understanding can be applied to sexual concerns.

Points to think about when considering working with a sex addicted client include the following:

• Clinicians who treat sex addiction need concrete knowledge about these disorders and the ways in which they can effectively be treated along with an extensive clinical understanding of human sexuality. Well meaning but untrained counselors can lack information about the types of sexual and romantic activities available through digital technology, or not know the right questions or the degree of inquiry required for assessment, thus tending to underestimate the profound effect of these activities on the day-to-day life of the addict. As a result, some therapists may attempt to make addicts more accepting of the behaviors, as in telling the compulsive masturbator that "masturbation is normal" without specifically addressing how masturbation works in that person's life, or by telling patients that they can keep hooking up using smartphone apps as long as they aren't hurting anyone. Therapists need to ask probing, specific but not necessarily graphic questions during assessment about the client's sexual and romantic activity. Only with a high level of detail from the start can a treatment professional gain the full picture of the issue and how it is affecting the client's life and the lives of those around the client.

- Therapists can err with sex and love addicts (or any active addict) when leaning into more traditional means of therapy—psychodynamic, narrative, Jungian, and trauma-based—as a primary initial form of work. When someone seeks therapy because they are feeling/acting out of control, it is the job of the therapist (following a solid assessment) to help the client stop his or her problematic activities in the here and now. And this work is best accomplished using highly directive techniques like CBT, behavioral contracts, accountability, psycho-education, directed reading, referrals to the right support groups, and homework assignments. By utilizing other treatment methods at the start, some therapists will inadvertently or unknowingly fail to make behavior change an early primary priority.

- Therapists working with a profoundly betrayed spouse or partner who seems "crazy" often fail to view these clients as people caught in a moment of crisis, instead erroneously viewing them as borderline or codependent. In reality, these are people who need help getting through their day more than anything else. As such, they need concrete direction in terms of healthcare, education, peer support, and more. What they don't need is to have their head examined, with a therapist focusing on their childhood or even a more current history of the couple's relationship.

- When a cybersex addict's behavior harms another person, such as his or her spouse or significant other, that person should, if at all possible, be brought into counseling as well. The therapist, even when not specifically doing couples work, can nonetheless offer help with boundaries, support, and direction.
- Always keep in mind the gold standard of our profession: If you are not fully familiar with a specific type of work or a particular client population, then you should make a referral or seek consultation. There are clinicians certified in the treatment of sex addiction who can guide you. Keep in mind that no therapist can do it all. Furthermore, none of us can be accused of malpractice or offering poor treatment (in the legal sense) as long as we can document that we have sought consultation with a knowledgeable professional.

Other Valuable Resources

- *Hypersexual Disorder: A Proposed Diagnosis for DSM-V,* by Martin P. Kafka, www.dsm5.org/Research/Documents/Kafka_Hypersexual_ASB.pdf
- International Institute for Trauma and Addiction Professionals, 480-575-6853, www.iitap.com
- National Council on Alcoholism and Drug Dependence, www.ncadd.org
- National Institute on Drug Abuse, www.drugabuse.gov
- Robert Weiss, www.robertweissmsw.com
- Sexual Addiction Resources, Dr. Patrick Carnes, www.sexhelp.com
- Sexual Recovery Institute, 877-959-4114, www.sexualrecovery.com
- Society for the Advancement of Sexual Health, 770-541-9912, www.sash.net
- Substance Abuse and Mental Health Services Administration, www.samsha.gov
- Jennifer Schneider, www.jenniferschneider.com
- Cybersex Addiction and Online Sex Offender Resources: Internet Behavior Consulting Company, 412-396-4032 www.internetbehavior.com

APPENDIX

ACTIVITY RESOURCES

THE SEXUAL BOUNDARY PLAN

The following are a few typical goals that underlie a sex addiction boundary plan. Your goals may (and probably will) differ in ways that reflect your values and circumstances.

1. I don't want to keep secrets from my spouse.

2. I want to have a real relationship with a real person, instead of just the online fantasies I've been having.

3. I want to feel like a whole person with integrity.

4. I want to be "present" in the real world instead of living half in this world and half in the cyber-world.

5. I want to regain trust with my partner and I don't want to put that trust at risk again.

6. I don't want to use pornography ever again.

7. I want to develop a healthy in-the-flesh sexual relationship with my lover.

Your goals will serve as overall guides to your sexual sobriety. Once they are defined, you can use them to help create your actual sexual boundary plan.

Some sexual sobriety plans start out as simple statements such as, "No viewing of sexual images or videos," or, "No going online or using my smartphone for any reason except to communicate with my family or for work," or, "I am sober as long as I do not pay for sex in any form." The important point here is to simply start somewhere and then be accountable to your plan by sharing it with a neutral person who is fully acquainted with your sexual and romantic history and issues. Over time, however, most people find they need a more elaborate set of guidelines to help steer their healing. Below is a description of such a plan, followed by a sample plan.

Part One: The Inner Boundary

The Inner Boundary is a bottom line definition of sexual sobriety, inclusive of concrete and specific behaviors (not thoughts or fantasies) that the addict wishes to stop. Placed within this boundary are the most damaging and troublesome acts. If addicts engage in any of these behaviors, they have had a slip and will need to restart their sobriety clock while thoroughly examining what led to the slip. Bottom line behaviors vary from person to person depending on whether someone is single, married, straight, gay, etc. Typical Inner Boundary behaviors include:

1. Going online for porn

2. Using smartphone sex locater apps

3. Having webcam sex

4. Paying for sex (including sensual massages)

5. Calling an ex for sex

6. Seeking any sex or romance outside one's primary relationship

Part Two: The Middle Boundary

The Middle Boundary addresses warning signs and slippery situations that can lead sex addicts back to their Inner Boundary behaviors. This boundary lists people, places, and experiences that could trigger the addict to act out. Again, these items are unique to each person. Included on this list are things indirectly related to acting out that may nevertheless trigger a desire to re-engage the addiction. Basically, anything that might cause a sex addict to want to dissociate and therefore return to Inner Boundary behaviors belongs in the Middle Boundary. Some typical Middle Boundary items include:

1. Overworking

2. Going online when alone

3. Using social media in secret

4. Disabling Internet filtering/accountability software

5. Reinstalling dating/hookup apps

6. Arguing with a spouse, significant other, boss, etc.

7. Skipping therapy or a support group

8. Lying

9. Practicing poor self-care (lack of sleep, eating poorly, not exercising, etc.)

10. Excessively worrying over finances

11. Traveling alone

12. Spending unstructured time alone

Part Three: The Outer Boundary

The Outer Boundary offers a vision for life improvements and positive things to come. It lists healthy activities, along with activities that lead people toward their life goals, hopes, and dreams. The items on this list may be immediate and concrete, such as "working on my house" and "spending more time with my kids," or long-term and less tangible, such as "beginning to understand my career goals" and "having a better relationship with my spouse." The list should reflect a healthy combination of work, recovery, and play. If going to a support group three times per week, exercising every day, and seeing a therapist once per week are on the list, then spending time with friends, going to the movies, and engaging in hobbies should also be listed. These healthy pleasures are the activities recovering people use to replace the intensity of acting out. Some typical Outer Boundary activities include:

1. Spending more time with my kids

2. Joining a writing group

3. Exercising daily

4. Getting a medical or dental checkup

5. Daily journaling and meditating

6. Working no more than eight hours a day

7. Keeping a clean house

8. Finding a new hobby, preferably one I can enjoy with family and friends

SAMPLE BOUNDARY PLAN

Sex and love addiction boundary plans vary according to the needs and life circumstances of the individual. Keep in mind that a single 23-year-old female sex addict will have a very different plan than a 55-year-old married guy with three kids. Hopefully, the following sample plan will help guide you in the creation of your own boundary plan. Some of the information included may seem redundant, but it is more helpful to be thorough and detailed in defining a plan than it is to be vague. Before implementing your boundary plan, you should always review it with at least one other person—your therapist, your Twelve Step recovery sponsor, or your accountability partner—and you should not change it later without consulting the individual who helped you develop it in the first place.

Partners and spouses are not the right people to turn to for help with your boundary plan, though they have every right to read it once it's completed. For spouses, the issues involved are far too personal and sensitive for them to be objective and truly helpful. Instead, the best person to help you establish your plan is someone who is knowledgeable about sex and love addiction, objective, and willing to stand up to you—a person who is not afraid of your anger or of hurting your feelings. These are people like trained sexual addiction therapists, faith-based leaders of sexual accountability groups, and Twelve Step sponsors.

GOALS

1. I don't want to use pornography or to have webcam sex ever again.
2. I don't want to keep secrets from my spouse.
3. I want to have a healthy relationship with my spouse and to eliminate the online fantasy relationships that I've been having.
4. I want to feel like a whole person with integrity.
5. I want to be "present" in the real world for my family, instead of constantly thinking about my "online life."
6. I want to regain trust with my spouse, and I don't want to put that trust at risk again.
7. I want to develop an enjoyable and rewarding sexual relationship with my spouse.

INNER BOUNDARIES (THE BOTTOM LINE)

1. No looking at any porn
2. No chat rooms (text or video)
3. No sex (online or in-the-flesh) with anyone other than my spouse
4. No texting, emailing, IMs, or sexting with past or potential romantic or sex partners
5. No masturbating alone

MIDDLE BOUNDARIES (WARNING SIGNS)

1. Going online when alone
2. Staying late at work
3. Visiting the app store when I'm alone
4. Keeping secrets
5. Not returning phone calls
6. Whole weekend open without plans
7. Fighting with my boss (or anyone else)
8. Not going to my support group
9. Not getting enough sleep
10. Skipping meals

OUTER BOUNDARIES (HEALTHY HEALING ACTIVITIES)

1. Attending Twelve Step meetings three times weekly
2. Going back to church
3. Volunteering to help with my kid's soccer practices
4. Forgetting about STD worries
5. Being on time
6. Exercising regularly
7. Joining the company softball team
8. Enjoying financial health and stability
9. Journaling and meditating daily

YOUR SEXUAL BOUNDARY PLAN

Now you are ready to create your own sexual boundary plan. You may utilize the space provided below, or you may create your plan on a separate sheet of paper or a digital device. Once it is complete, review this plan with your accountability partner. You will need to approve it together, and you will each sign it, showing your commitment to upholding it and your accountability partner's commitment to helping you. The date you sign the plan is your sobriety date. Every day that you don't engage in an Inner Boundary behavior, you are sober.

Once your plan is signed, changes cannot be made to it without first discussing the matter with your accountability partner. Remember, it is best if your accountability partner is either a therapist specializing in sexual addiction or your sponsor from a Twelve Step sex addiction recovery program.

My Goals
(overall guides to my sexual boundary plan)

1. . . . .

2. . . . .

3. . . . .

4. . . . .

5. . . . .

6. . . . .

My Inner Boundaries
(the sexual behaviors I want to stop)

1. . . . .

2. . . . .

3. . . . .

4. . . . .

5. . . . .

6. . . . .

MY MIDDLE BOUNDARIES
(warning signs and slippery situations)

1. . . . .

2. . . . .

3. . . . .

4. . . . .

5. . . . .

6. . . . .

7. . . . .

8. . . . .

9. . . . .

10. . . . .

11. . . . .

12. . . . .

MY OUTER BOUNDARIES
(positive rewards and ways to maintain my sexual boundaries)

1. . . . .

2. . . . .

3. . . . .

4. . . . .

5. . . . .

6. . . . .

7. . . . .

8. . . . .

9. . . . .

10. . . . .

11. . . . .

12. . . . .

My signature: . . . .

My accountability partner's signature: . . . .

Date: . . . .

A FEW TIPS ON SEXUAL BOUNDARY PLANS

1. Remember that a boundary plan is meant to hold you accountable to your commitments, particularly in the face of challenging circumstances. Unless you have clearly written boundaries in your recovery plan, you are vulnerable to deciding in the moment what choices are best—and, unfortunately, most such impulsive decisions are not conducive to sexual or romantic sobriety.

2. Bear in mind that boundary plans can be flexible over time. Recovering people often spend a month or two with a particular set of boundaries and then wonder if they need adjustment. However, changing a boundary plan is not something you should do on your own; making changes involves engaging the help of someone who fully understands your problems and their context (your

accountability partner). Changes to a boundary plan should never be made just because some special situation presents itself and you decide, in the moment, that it is time to make a change. That is not called changing your plan; it's called acting out.

3. If you are looking to justify the continuation of a particular behavior, even though you know deep down it is not right and no longer serves a healthy purpose, you can nearly always find someone to sign off on that, to agree that it was "never a big deal anyway." It is important to remember that the purpose of creating a boundary plan is not to justify or rationalize previous behaviors (or a version thereof); the purpose is to stop acting out.

4. If you are in a relationship, consider how your new boundaries will affect your spouse or significant other. For instance, a period of total abstinence for you may also affect your partner significantly. Your partner may already be feeling sexually rejected by you. Talk to your partner about your decision to commit to a period of total abstinence and the duration of that period. If your partner is uncomfortable with your decision, then the two of you should discuss it with a couples therapist knowledgeable about sex addiction.

Developing a Dating Plan

Reviewing sample dating plans may help you learn new, healthier dating habits. The following plan will not reflect everyone's needs, as it is written for a person whose primary acting out behavior was hooking up for anonymous sex using smartphone apps. Nevertheless, as a typical example it can help you devise your own dating plan. You should not develop your dating plan on your own. Instead, work with your therapist, your sponsor, or your supportive friends in recovery. Furthermore, you should not change this plan without first consulting the person or people who helped you construct it.

Sample Dating Plan

1. I don't have sex until after at least the third date.

2. I don't have sex during the first three weeks of knowing someone new.

3. On the first date, we will stay in public places.

4. I don't date anyone I wouldn't introduce to friends.

5. I don't date anyone who is in a relationship with someone else.

6. I don't date anyone who is actively using hard drugs.

The goal of the dating plan is to help you learn how to get to know a person before becoming sexual or deeply infatuated. This supports your personal growth because you begin to base your sexual and romantic choices not only on whether the person is exciting, but also on whether you like something about who that person is. If you're a sex addict, a well-thought-out dating plan helps you curtail your initial impulse to have sex before you get to know the other person. If you're love addicted, a dating plan can quash your initial impulse to fall head over heels in love before getting to know the other person.

> *The dating part isn't so hard. I go out for coffee with a guy and see how we get along. If he's cute and if it works out, next time we do a movie or dinner. The difficult part is that once I sit down and start talking to some of these guys—I mean really talking—my desire to sleep with them gets less and less intense. Most of them are fine until they open their mouths, and then I realize they don't have much to say. Or maybe they have a lot to say, but none of it interests me.*

> *Since my dating plan says that I need to have three dates before having sex, I find that I just don't have that much sex. I've found in recovery that I really need to be stimulated by what a guy has to say before I want to be sexual with him. I know this is funny, but I never knew this before. When I was having anonymous sex, no one ever said anything—everything took place in silence. No wonder I could never make any of those situations work out.*

> —Mark, thirty-one, bartender

Now you are ready to create your own dating plan. You may utilize the space provided below, or you may create your plan on a separate sheet of paper or a digital device. As you're writing, keep in mind your goals for personal growth as well as your past history of acting out. Once your plan is complete, review it with your accountability partner. You will need to approve it together, and you will each sign it, showing your commitment to upholding it and your accountability partner's commitment to helping you.

My Personal Dating Plan:

1. . . . .

2. . . . .

3. . . . .

4. . . . .

5. . . . .

6. . . . .

7. . . . .

8. . . . .

My signature: . . . .

My accountability partner's signature: . . . .

Date: . . . .

Advanced Dating Plans

If you're struggling to formulate a dating plan, an exercise you may find helpful is the establishment of dating traffic signals—red lights, yellow lights, and green lights. These markers are designed to help you see who is a good person to date and who is bound to disappoint you. It is wise to review this list with someone—most likely your therapist or you sponsor— who can help you evaluate whether your expectations are reasonable, and whether you're overselling or shortchanging yourself.

Red Lights: These are characteristics or qualities that are *unacceptable to me* in anyone I might date. I would stop seeing a person who is:

1. An active alcoholic, drug addict, sex addict, or love addict

2. Still in a primary romantic relationship with someone else

3. Still living with an ex after they have broken up

4. Someone who lies to me

5. Someone who doesn't return my phone calls, texts, or emails

6. Unemployed with no means of income other than a weekly unemployment check

Yellow Lights: These characteristics or qualities might present a problem when I observe them in someone I am dating. I'll be cautious if he or she:

1. Talks, especially about himself or herself, a lot more than he or she listens

2. Recently ended a long-term relationship

3. Only seems to call me when he or she wants or needs something

4. Doesn't make me feel safe or appreciated when we're together

5. Makes me handle all the plans and contacts for socializing

6. Doesn't offer to pay for meals or dates

7. Doesn't seem to want me to meet any of his or her friends, or doesn't seem to want to meet any of my friends

8. Doesn't want to plan ahead, and often reschedules or cancels plans we've made

Green Lights: These are characteristics or qualities in a potential romantic partner that I really like and find attractive. I would be encouraged to continue dating a person who:

1. Tries to find out what is going on with me and how I am doing

2. Offers to help me out with things I am doing

3. Surprises me with fun or playful experiences

4. Has interesting hobbies and displays his or her own sense of creativity

5. Shares interests with me

6. Returns calls, texts, and emails in a reasonable amount of time and shows up for things we've planned to do

By outlining the positive and negative signs that alert you to various issues in dating and new relationships, you offer yourself a better opportunity for objective reflection when you're caught up in the excitement of meeting someone new. Having a solid dating plan and clearly delineated traffic signals to rely on makes it less likely that you will lose track of yourself in the intensity of the moment or become involved in painful or addictive relationships.

While non-addicts may have the common sense to recognize intuitively these red and yellow light problems and potential problems and respond to them in healthy ways, sex addicts need rational, well-defined guidelines to keep themselves grounded. Although these basic boundaries may seem obvious and overly simplistic, they can help you successfully establish and maintain balanced relationships and genuine affection. Over time, as your romantic relationships become more selective and less casual, you'll begin to develop a better sense of whom to choose as a romantic or sexual partner, and you'll reflexively make healthier and safer choices about the people you date. Until that point in time, though, creating and customizing your plan will help you to find and stay on the path of healthy dating.

Now you are ready to create your own dating plan. You may utilize the space provided here, or you may create your plan on a separate sheet of paper or a digital device.

RED LIGHTS: END IT NOW!

1. . . . .

2. . . . .

3. . . . .

4. . . . .

5. . . . .

6. . . . .

YELLOW LIGHTS: PROCEED WITH CAUTION

1. . . . .

2. . . . .

3. . . . .

4. . . . .

5. . . . .

6. . . . .

GREEN LIGHTS: MOVE FORWARD

1. . . . .

2. . . . .

3. . . . .

4. . . . .

5. . . . .

6. . . . .

NOTES

PREFACE

1. Jennifer Schneider and Robert Weiss, *Cybersex Exposed: Simple Fantasy or Obsession?* (Center City, MN: Hazelden, 2001).

2. Robert Weiss and Jennifer Schneider, *Untangling the Web: Sex, Porn, and Fantasy Obsession in the Digital Age* (Center City, MN: Hazelden, 2006).

3. Robert Weiss and Jennifer Schneider, *Closer Together, Further Apart: the Effect of Technology and the Internet on Parenting, Work, and Relationships* (Carefree, AZ: Gentle Path Press, 2014).

4. Ami Sedghi, "Facebook: 10 Years of Social Networking, in Numbers," *The Guardian*, accessed May 27, 2014, http://www.theguardian.com/news/datablog/2014/feb/04/facebook-in-numbers-statistics.

INTRODUCTION

1. "The Internet Big Picture: World Internet Users and Population Stats," Internet World Stats, accessed June 30, 2012, http://www.internetworldstats.com/stats.htm.

2. David Levy, *Love and Sex with Robots: The Evolution of Human-Robot Relationships* (New York: HarperCollins Publishers, 2007), 22.

3. Ibid., 9.

CHAPTER ONE

1. A. Cooper, D. E. Putman, L. A. Planchon, and S. C. Boies, "Online Sexual Compulsivity: Getting Tangled in the Net," *Sexual Addiction and Compulsivity* 6 (1999): 79–104.

2. Dhawal Damania, "Internet Pornography Statistics," accessed May 28, 2014, http://thedinfographics.com/2011/12/23/internet-pornography-statistics/.

3. Cooper, et. al. "Online Sexual Compulsivity: Getting Tangled in the Net."

4. Philip Zimbardo and Nikita Duncan. *The Demise of Guys: Why Boys Are Struggling and What We Can Do About It* (2012).

5. Gary Wilson, "Why Shouldn't Johnny Watch Porn if He Likes?" Your Brain on Porn, accessed August 21, 2014, http://yourbrainonporn.com/why-shouldnt-johnny-watch-porn-if-he-likes.

6. Damania. "Internet Pornography Statistics."

7. Candice Odgers, Avshalom Caspi, Daniel Nagin, Alex Piquero, Wendy Slutske, Barry Milne, Nigel Dickson, Richie Poulton, and Terrie Moffitt, "Is It Important to Prevent Early Exposure to Drugs and Alcohol among Adolescents?" *Psychological Science* 19 (10): 1037–44.

8. Gary Wilson, "Kids and Porn: It Ain't Your Father's Playboy," Your Brain on Porn, accessed June 2, 2014, http://yourbrainonporn.com/boys-and-porn-it-aint-your-fathers-playboy.

9. Al Cooper, "Sexuality and the Internet: Surfing into the New Millennium." *CyberPsychology & Behavior* 1 (1998): 187–93.

Chapter Two

1. Martin P. Kafka, "Hypersexual Disorder: A Proposed Diagnosis for DSM-V." *Archives of Sexual Behavior* 39 (2010): 377-400.

2. Ibid.

3. R. Reid, B. Carpenter, J. Hook, S. Garos, J. Manning, R. Gilliland, T. Fong, "Report of Findings in a DSM-5 Field Trial for Hypersexual Disorder," *The Journal of Sexual Medicine* 11 (2012): 2868-2877.

4. V. Voon and T. Mole, "Neural Correlates of Sexual Cue Reactivity in Individuals With and Without Compulsive Sexual Behaviours," *Plos One,* 10 (2014): 1371.

5. "Definition of Addiction," American Society of Addiction Medicine, accessed August 20, 2014, http://www.asam.org/for-the-public/definition-of-addiction.

6. Tara Berman, "Sexual Addiction May Be Real After All," *ABC News*, accessed August 20, 2014, http://abcnews.go.com/blogs/health/2014/07/11/sexual-addiction-may-be-real-after-all/.

Chapter Three

1. J. P. Schneider, "Effects of Cybersex Addiction on the Family: Results of a Survey," *Sexual Addiction and Compulsivity* 7 (2000): 31–58.

2. Gary Wilson, "What Experts Tell Guys Suffering from ED," Your Brain on Porn, accessed June 3, 2014, http://yourbrainonporn.com/what-experts-tell-guys-suffering-from-ed.

3. Roger Pulvers, "Reversing Japan's Rising Sex Aversion May Depend on a Rebirth of Hope," *The Japan Times*, April 29, 2102, http://www.japantimes.co.jp/text/fl20120429rp.html.

4. J. P. Schneider, R. Weiss, and C. Samenow, "Is It Really Cheating? Understanding the Emotional Reactions and Clinical Treatment of Spouses and Partners Affected by Cybersex Infidelity," *Sexual Addiction & Compulsivity* 19 (2012): 123–39.

CHAPTER FOUR

1. Patrick Carnes. *Don't Call It Love: Recovery from Sexual Addiction* (New York: Bantam, 1992).
2. J. P. Schneider, "A Qualitative Study of Cybersex Participants: Gender Differences, Recovery Issues, and Implications for Therapists," *Sexual Addiction & Compulsivity* 7 (2000): 249–78.
3. B. Traeen, T. Sorheim Nilsen, and H. Stigum, "Use of Pornography in Traditional Media and on the Internet in Norway," *Journal of Sex Research* 43 (2006): 245–54.
4. Damania, "Internet Pornography Statistics."
5. M.C. Ferree, "Women and the Web: Cybersex Activity and Implications," *Sexual and Relationship Therapy (2003) 18(3): 385-393.*

CHAPTER SIX

1. S. Carnes and M. Lee, "Picking Up the Pieces, Helping Partners and Family Members," chap. 11 in *Behavioral Addictions: Criteria, Evidence, and Treatment* (Waltham, MA: Academic Press, 2014), 270-271.
2. B. A. Steffens and R. L. Rennie, "The Traumatic Nature of Disclosure for Wives of Sexual Addicts," *Sexual Addiction & Compulsivity* 13 (2006): 247–67.
3. The concept of gaslighting as a part of betrayal trauma has evolved from the clinical work of Omar Minwalla, Jerry Goodman, and Sylvia Jackson.
4. Schneider, Weiss, and Samenow, "Is It Really Cheating?"
5. Barbara Steffens and Marsha Means, *Your Sexually Addicted Spouse: How Partners Can Hope and Heal* (Far Hills, NJ: New Horizons Press, 2009).
6. Schneider, Weiss, and Samenow, "Is It Really Cheating?"
7. M. D. Corley, J. P. Schneider, and J. N. Hook, "Partner Reactions to Disclosure of Relapse by Self-Identified Sexual Addicts," *Sexual Addiction & Compulsivity* 19 (2012): 265–83.

CHAPTER SEVEN

1. Kenneth Adams, *Silently Seduced: When Parents Make Their Children Partners* (Deerfield Beach, FL: Health Communications, 1991).
2. Emily Bazelon, "What Really Happened to Phoebe Prince?" *Slate,* accessed June 6, 2014, http://www.slate.com/articles/life/bulle/features/2010/what_really_happened_to_phoebe_prince/the_untold_story_of_her_suicide_and_the_role_of_the_kids_who_have_been_criminally_charged_for_it.html.
3. J. Wolak, D. Finkelhor, K. Mitchell, and M. Ybarra, "Online Predators and Their Victims: Myths, Realities, and Implications for Prevention and Treatment," *American Psychologist* (2008) 63: 111–28.

CHAPTER ELEVEN

1. Corley, Schneider, and Hook, "Partner Reactions to Disclosure of Relapse by Self-Identified Sexual Addicts."

OTHER BOOKS BY ROBERT WEISS AND JENNIFER SCHNEIDER

Closer Together, Further Apart: The Effect of Technology and the Internet on Parenting, Work, and Relationships

Other books by Robert Weiss
Cruise Control: Understanding Sex Addiction in Gay Men

Sex Addiction 101: A Basic Guide to Healing from Sex, Porn, and Love Addiction

Other books by Jennifer Schneider
Back from Betrayal: Recovering from His Affairs

Disclosing Secrets: An Addict's Guide for When, to Whom, and How Much to Reveal (with Deborah Corley)

Embracing Recovery from Chemical Dependency: A Personal Recovery Plan (with Deborah Corley and Richard Irons)

Living with Chronic Pain: The Complete Health Guide to the Causes and Treatment of Chronic Pain

Sex, Lies, and Forgiveness: Couples Speak Out on Healing from Sex Addiction (with Burt Schneider)

Surviving Disclosure: A Partner's Guide for Healing the Betrayal of Intimate Trust (with Deborah Corley)

The Wounded Healer: An Addiction-Sensitive Approach to the Sexually Exploitative Professional (with Richard Irons)

Understand Yourself, Understand Your Partner: The Essential Enneagram Guide to a Better Relationship (with Ron Corn)

ABOUT THE AUTHORS

Robert Weiss LCSW, CSAT-S, is an author, clinical trainer, addiction psychotherapist and authority on the interaction of digital technology with sexual health, relationships and addiction. Currently serving as Senior Vice-President of Clinical Development for Elements Behavioral Health, Mr. Weiss has developed ongoing clinical addiction treatment programs for The Ranch in Nunnelly, TN, Promises Treatment Centers in Malibu, CA, The Sexual Recovery Institute in Los Angeles, CA (founded by Mr. Weiss in 1995) and the Life Healing Center of Santa Fe, NM. Mr. Weiss is a licensed, UCLA MSW graduate and early trainee of Dr. Patrick Carnes, an international leader in addiction treatment. He is the author of four books, numerous peer-reviewed articles, and book chapters.

Mr. Weiss has served as a media specialist in the area of sex addiction and the role of digital technology in our relationships for CNN, the Oprah Winfrey Network, the *New York Times, LA Times* and the *Today* show, *Dateline NBC* among many others. He contributes regularly to PsychCentral.com, writing primarily about sex addiction, and the Huffington Post, writing mostly about the effects of technology on communication and intimacy in relationships. Mr. Weiss has also provided clinical multi-addiction training and behavioral health program development for the National Institutes of Health, the United States military along with multiple behavioral health centers throughout the United States, Europe and Asia.

Jennifer P. Schneider, MD, PhD, is a physician certified in internal medicine, addiction medicine and pain management. She is the author of fourteen books, several chapters, and numerous articles in professional journals. She is a nationally recognized expert in two addiction-related fields: addictive sexual disorders and the management of chronic pain with opioids. Now retired from direct patient care, her professional activities include writing, lecturing at conferences, serving as an expert witness in legal settings, and appearing as a media guest on television and radio.